Buttons in My Soup:

The story of
a Buchenwald survivor

Moshe Ziv (Zisovitch)

Translated from Hebrew by Sharolyn Buxbaum

We would like to extend our heartfelt gratitude to Sharolyn.
Thank you for your initiative, your wise guidance and your
generous support.

Edited by Eliora Sivan-Zohar

Thank you Eliora for your dedicated, diligent and
meticulous work.
Your sensitive treatment of the text was matched only by your
professional skill.

With our utmost thanks
Nika, Ronen and Vardit Ziv

2019

To my dear wife Nika,
thank you from the bottom of my heart!

During our marriage of 42 years I shared with you quite
a lot about my life "there". These were episodes and
fragments I remembered as I went about my daily life. Nika,
and my children Vardit and Ronen, you always listened to
my stories and found them interesting, even though they
were often just partial memories. I agreed to try, and with
your ongoing encouragement indeed succeeded in recording
almost my complete life story.

I thank you Nika for your great effort, and for the countless
nights you spent deciphering my handwriting and helping
me bring this book to print.

Moshe Ziv (Zisovitch)

Table of Contents

In 1938 a military pact was signed between the leader of Hungary, Admiral Miklos Horthy, and the chancellor of Germany, Adolf Hitler. As a reward, territory taken from Hungary under the Treaty of Versailles following World War I was returned to the country. At the time the "Jewish question" was debated in the Hungarian parliament and a series of racial laws was legislated.

In 1940, all Jews who had served in the Hungarian army during World War I, including my father, were sent to forced labor battalions. In 1943, a law exiling foreign citizens was passed, mainly affecting the Jewish population. One year later, more than 600,000 Hungarian Jews were sent to extermination camps.

I was liberated from the Buchenwald concentration camp on April 11, 1945. In the decades that followed I made notes and partial journal entries as I recalled the events. Following the second international meeting of the "Buchenwald Boys" in April 1990)in Tel Aviv(, and with the encouragement of my family, I decided to turn my notes into a book. In the course of my writing I discovered that I had no need for notes or reminders. Much time had elapsed, almost 50 years, but most of the events were fresh in my memory, and I would not forget them until my last day.

There, far to the East, in a peaceful spring scene
There, black furrows to be planted
There, a horizon blue and pure,
There, a song of spring was severed.
There, in the East, only a shattering cry is heard,
There my father and mother, and all ended in silence.
No scream and no voice. Everything is quiet and still.
The heavens are locked and sealed.
Just lowering clouds, loaded with sparks, that's all!
Everything is still, the barracks are dark,
On the horizon just the chimneys of Birkenau glow
And the smoke continues to rise, hovering over all
Like a weighty beam, threatening from above in
its heaviness.
The air is scorched, sparks float down. Hot!
Breathing is hard, rattled.
My father holds my hand: Look, we are still here! Over
there, my son, they are only burning waste from the cars.
- My father, over there thousands are being destroyed
each day!
- My precious son, my innocent one, we are here.
When summer came, my father left and did not return.

1.

Childhood

All is silent, still and daunting in the emptiness. There is neither sky nor horizon. Heavy clouds hang over us. Thick smoke curls upward from four corners. Is this what Hell looks like? A huge square stretches before us, only black asphalt up to the horizon and a barbed-wire fence all around up to the sky. Everything, like the smoke, is very precise and symmetrical ... around me there are thousands of people in striped clothing. Everything is blue and white. This time I am a prisoner with a real identity; this time the Germans kept their promise. I had heard about the "resettlement" for many months. And today, I am on a different planet.

Two hours ago we had gotten off the freight train cars. In my car there were close to one hundred people. For a moment I forgot the gnawing hunger inside. A week ago we had been loaded onto the freight cars. My father and I had received two loaves of bread for the journey. My father wanted to be careful: we wolfed down only one loaf of bread on the first day of the journey, saving the other. It was wonderful: fresh bread with a flaky crust...

My father hid the second loaf in his knapsack, where he kept just a few things we had managed to pack at the previous camp – Sárvár Camp in western Hungary near the Austrian border. It was terribly crowded on the train. I clung to my father. We sat in silence, with nothing to talk about.

I understood very well that there was no point in asking questions, because no one knew where we were going. I felt rather safe because of the calming things we had been told by the various Jewish workers at the previous camp. I had yet to understand what awaited us at the "resettlement".

From time to time panic broke out in the packed car. A Jew would faint and would be moved to the corner of the car. Before the first night was over we had grown accustomed to the sight of piles of people stacked up in the corners, and we could not tell if they were dead or alive.

In the passageways, near the doors, two SS men sat and kept things quiet. When the train stopped at a station those near the doors were made to empty the overflowing latrine pails. It was rumored that the SS men had a separate car in the train. From time to time we heard bursts of gunshots: were they meant to frighten us?

At each station we were given less water. The tracks were loaded with trains carrying soldiers equipped for battle. Two or three times a day our train was sidetracked to enable the army to pass.

From time to time the local farmers would come to our cars and hand us bottles of water, receiving in return watches, rings and other jewelry. We did not understand how they knew that Jews were being transported in the trains. Sometimes the farmers would take the jewelry but then maliciously spill the water. I have no doubt that the Christian population was very satisfied that the Jews were being sent for extermination. Perhaps they did not know for sure where the Jews were being sent, but they were undoubtedly eager to get their hands on Jewish property by any means, even alongside the freight cars. I had already experienced their hatred as a young boy.

Since my father and I had no rings to exchange we did not get close to the barred windows. I sat hunched beside my father, and the only complaint I had was the smell of garlic and sausage from someone near me. That person wrapped his head in a heavy coat to muffle the sounds of his chewing. Pangs of hunger ran through me, but I kept quiet. My father promised me that we would eat the second loaf of bread the next day.

We left Hungary, traveling northeast. I tried to guess where we were going. Rumor had it that it was Poland, but we knew nothing for certain. I was tired and depleted. We had been in transit for three days. The elderly and exhausted were pushed into the corner; most were unconscious. Near the barred windows was a small empty area where we could take turns getting some air. Every two or three hours I would go there to breathe fresh air. We passed by oak forests, vast expanses with no trace of human life. As I stood at the barred window I dreamt that I was on a school outing in the forests near my birthplace, Miskolc…dozing and nodding I also dreamt of sausages we roasted over the bonfire. Every time I dreamt of taking the first bite I awoke and felt awful. Disappointed, I returned to sit beside my father.

The next morning we decided to eat the second loaf of bread, but soon discovered what a mistake we had made hiding it so well. The bread that had been fresh three days ago was now mildewed and rubbery, unpleasant to touch. We managed to eat some of the crust but had to throw out what was left. Later I would regret the delicacy we had thrown away, since we received no other food for the rest of the journey. Our hunger grew stronger. I lost my sense of time and place. No one spoke to his neighbor. Like me, they understood that when we arrived at our destination, wherever it would be, not many would be able to get off the train on their own.

What do people think about, hunched over, side by side, day after day? Perhaps I will tell my father how bitter I had felt during the four years preceding this transport? Better not; I can feel how worried he is. He continually caresses and squeezes my hand.

"Father", I say, "my watch has stopped".

"Give it to me", father says. I hand him the watch, the first watch I had ever owned, and father takes it and puts it in his pocket. "When we come back, I'll take it to be fixed", he says.

The second precious item of mine is in my father's knapsack. In a carefully wrapped package were pieces of cloth cut to my measurements. They were supposed to be sewn into a sports suit for me, and beside them in a basket were the buttons and stiffened lapels. I was supposed to get the suit when I was 15, two years after my *Bar Mitzvah* [1], but because of the rumors of a transport the tailor had returned the pieces of material to us before using them to sew my suit. The watch and the suit, two dream items from my former life…

Did my father know about the hard years we endured up to now, while he was away serving in the Hungarian army? Those were crazy years, not really life, years of want and unrelenting persecution by the Hungarian fascists. What did my father know about this? Actually, there was no point in saying anything, since nothing would be as it had been before.

Chopped Meat

Until I was ten my life was altogether normal, as was the life of most of the Jewish community in Miskolc. Living close to my mother's extended family, in the heart of the large Jewish neighborhoods in the city, I recall the holidays we celebrated with all the relatives as pleasant occasions, sometimes a little stormy. There was continuous tension between my mother and her brothers-in-law, because she was the only daughter who observed all 613 *mitzvot* (Jewish commandments) and followed

---

[1] *Bar Mitzvah* – a coming of age Jewish ritual when a Jewish boy turns 13.

a Jewish way of life in every sense of the word (similar to that of the extremely religious Neturei Karta Jews). Up until the war broke out my education consisted of a half day of secular studies and a half day in a *Cheder* [2], where Jewish boys like me studied Judaic texts and Hebrew.

With the outbreak of war groups of fanatic youth began persecuting Jews in every possible way. Life in the Jewish neighborhoods became a nightmare. I recall my childhood years as a continuing series of maneuvering and dodging whenever I came home from school or left the *Cheder*. Gangs of Christian teens attacked us from every direction. Sometimes a group of older Jewish boys would wait at a street corner to give them a taste of their own medicine, but that was like a drop in the ocean. Anyway, life went on. In hindsight I don't know what was worse for me, the poverty at home or the terror on the streets and in the neighborhood.

After my father had been away for two years I allowed myself more and more freedom. By the time I was twelve I sometimes gave myself permission to befriend Christian boys. The source of the temptation was the acute lack of food. More than once I was tempted to eat non-*kosher*[3] food at their homes, even though I felt that their willingness to offer it did not stem from their generosity but rather from the satisfaction of successfully tempting a Jewish boy to eat pork. While eating their food I feared the punishment that would befall me from the heavens above. My good mother could instinctively tell when I had eaten outside our home. She would always caress my head and promise that nothing bad would happen to me and that God would watch over me. There was a time when I truly believed that because of my mother's piousness everything would turn out all right.

---

[2] *Cheder* - A Jewish religious classroom where Jewish boys study Judaic texts and Hebrew.

[3] *Kosher* - foods that conform to a set of Jewish religious dietary laws. In slang may also mean "proper" or "legitimate".

I do not know what sustained us until my father returned from the army. Apparently we lived off the last bit of my mother's small savings. I remembered *Rosh Hashanah* [4], the Jewish New Year in 1941, when lack of funds was so severe that we did not have the money to buy the tiny amount of rationed food distributed during the war. For days I dragged my feet from one grocery store to another, and mostly stood in front of the large Christian butcher shop on the main street, where I counted the meatballs in two big bowls displayed in the window. The big fat butcher would stand in the doorway and smile with delight at the sight of the little Jewish boy with his *peyes* [5].

"Nu, boy, do you want a pork meatball?" he asked. I did not answer, only crossed over to the other side of the main street, my mouth watering and my stomach growling from hunger.

On the eve of *Rosh Hashanah* I came home and caught my breath in surprise. The dinner table was loaded with holiday dishes. Everything I had dreamt of was there on the table: all except meatballs. I asked my mother to make a big bowl of meatballs. "Moshe-Yankel, why do we need meatballs for Rosh Hashanah? Look, we have plenty of holiday food, what made you think of meatballs?" she inquired.

Of course I did not tell her about my wandering in the Christian street… and after my initial surprise I understood the source of the food. When I went into the bedroom I found an empty saucer on the closet shelf, and I knew very well that something was missing there. I remembered that a crown had fallen off my mother's tooth, and she had been waiting for a chance to have it put back. Now I understood: mother had sold the gold crown so that she could prepare food for the holiday.

I loved my mother very much, and I tried to do what

---

[4]   *Rosh Hashanah* - Jewish New Year.
[5]   *Peyes*, or *payot* – the sidelocks of ultra-Orthodox men and boys, in keeping with the Torah's prohibition of shaving the "corners" of the head.

she wanted and study the Torah. Sometimes I would ask her embarrassing questions about religion, questions that came up because of our continuous distress and lack at home. Mother would listen patiently and tell me about famous rabbis who helped people in need, stories about the Messiah who would come, about an abundance of food that would fall from the heavens and about the enormous Leviathan that would supply meat to all the people of Israel. The stories enchanted me, especially when she told them at the end of Shabbat while we waited for the three stars that signaled the end of the Sabbath to appear. Later, in the lamplight, things seemed much gloomier. Not much food was left over from the Shabbat meal and what remained was kept for tomorrow's dinner.

In the autumn of 1942 rumors had spread that mobilized men over the age of 42 would be released from the army. Ever since Father was drafted, in 1938 at the age of 38, we had heard very little from him, mostly printed postcards with the message "I am well" over his signature. At least it was some sign of life. The same year hundreds of Jewish refugees reached Miskolc from lands conquered by the Nazis. I don't know how or why they came to Hungary, perhaps because at the time no one knew that the Jews of Hungary would be washed into the same river of blood, that the same fate awaited them. Among the refugees were well-known rabbis from Poland, including the Rabbi of Belz. As a 14-year old religious Jewish boy I admired his famous personality, although there were things that I did not understand. My mother could barely scrape together enough money to get an appointment with the rabbi and hand him a *kvitel*[6], a note of supplications, so that he would pray to God on behalf of our family, especially for my father to return home quickly. My grandmother, my mother's mother, lived not far from us with my unmarried aunt. Unlike my mother, my aunt was far removed from religion and only

[6] *Kvitel* - a note written by an individual with a petitionary prayer given to the Rabbi in order to receive his blessing.

observed the commandments she absolutely had to. In the summertime I was happy to run errands between my mother and my grandmother. I don't remember how old I was when this arrangement began, but I remember very well that when I was twelve I could not take my eyes off my aunt sunbathing in the back yard, dark as a Gypsy.

Family arguments in those years also included some discussion about my *peyes*, since they identified me as a Jew. One day, when I returned from school, my aunt "evened" one side of my *peyes*, with the excuse that one was longer than the other. Of course my mother was forced to "even out" the other one, as if she silently agreed to get rid of my *peyes*. Life on the street was easier for me after that: the Christian bullies attacked me less frequently.

At that time gangs of Arrow Cross, the Hungarian fascist party, ran wild in the city streets, rounding up Jews for forced labor and vandalizing their stores. It seemed that the entire city was happy to support these gangs. Towards winter we reached our last crumbs of bread. My mother was a proud woman. When I visited my aunts, who were better off than us because their husbands were not drafted, my mother had me mind my manners and refuse whatever food was offered. I could not always resist temptation, and when they offered a second time I would accept. According to the level of eagerness I exhibited before our meal at home my mother knew whether I had found food elsewhere. For several months now we had become accustomed to eating our meal at night so as not to go to bed on an empty stomach. We would stand beside the stove in the evening, waiting for the potatoes to cook. My sister Kati and I would peel and slice the potatoes, placing them in the bowl. The main flavoring for the dish was duck fat.

I would also run errands for my aunts, since adults stayed off the streets. I was the one who brought the news and rumors back to the family. One winter evening, when I was on my way back from *Ma'ariv* [7] evening prayers, (which was my way of compensating my mother for the ever-growing times I avoided going to the *Cheder*) I told my mother about groups of people standing in line outside the Jewish community offices, waiting for aid packages. My mother warned me not to go there. "We don't need charity", she said forcefully.

I did not tell my mother that the place was full of people, including many boys my age from among our acquaintances. The following days I continued to see the lines. One time I saw a beautiful woman with curly blonde hair standing by one of the tables where parcels were being distributed. I stared at her, because in our observant neighborhood where I grew up women were not seen with their head uncovered. I don't know why she returned my glance. Once she called me over to tell me to wait until all those in line had received their parcels.

The Jewish community office building had central heating. I felt wonderful as I waited. I even forgot that I had not eaten since morning. I walked up and down the hall without knowing why I was waiting. Once in a while I would peek into the office to see if the line was gone. It was getting dark outside and I needed to get home so my mother would not worry. I knocked on the office door. The blonde woman greeted me with a big smile: "I am sure you would like to drink a glass of warm milk" she said to me (I hated milk). This was the first time I was near a woman who did not resemble those in our neighborhood. She warmed up some milk and went around the room tidying up the desks. The smell of the perfume wafting from her roused my imagination and made me think of the movies I had seen without permission. She served me the glass of milk with a white napkin. I was not naturally shy, but I had never stood so close to an unfamiliar woman. My eyes went from her face, to her neck, to her flowered blouse, unbuttoned where a string of pearls adorned her neck. Not breathing, I did not take my eyes off of her.

---

[7] *Ma'ariv* – evening prayer in Judaism.

"Nice boy, come again tomorrow. We'll find you a good jacket in the storeroom.", she told me as I left.

I don't know how I got home considering my state of confusion. I was sure that everyone could smell perfume on me.

Deportation

As winter approached rumors of my father's return increased. I gave a lot of thought to what I would do when he came home. I remembered him as a broad-shouldered man, not hunched over like most of the men I saw around me. Most of the Jews walked close to the buildings in constant fear. The sight of a Jew walking on the sidewalk and being rudely pushed to the side by young thugs was an everyday event, as were Jews being beaten and abused and their beards ripped off.

Finally the day came when my father returned home.

I thought that many things would now go back to being as they were before he left, but actually everything changed. My father was only forty-two years old but his hair had turned white. He was quiet, depressed, and kept to himself. What could I ask him? He asked us very little about our life and did not pressure me to study religion fervently. He concentrated on one thing: finding work. There was no employment in the business he had worked in before the war. There was nothing left but to search for day jobs. By now there were still some warehouses and factories owned jointly by Christians and Jews. My father found a day job at one of these places, but this did not improve our economic situation much. Every day I saw him leave for work with a package wrapped in a white napkin.

One day my curiosity got the better of me, only to discover that the pretty package contained nothing but bread. "Why, isn't there something else in the house to eat?" I asked. My mother explained that father would leave that "something else" for the children.

My mother told me that father had a hard time falling asleep at night as he talked about what happened during his army service. I was curious and decided to eavesdrop on his stories. They sounded as if they were straight out of a horror story! Stories of the mass slaughter of Jews and accounts of the Jewish labor battalion whose job it was to dig mass graves for Jews being slaughtered!

Throughout the time my father was drafted I was the family representative, going to the police every few months to renew our papers. I would always invent an illness to explain what had prevented my mother from coming and why I had come instead. Very few Jews dared to go to the Hungarian authorities to arrange their affairs, and my mother felt that it would be better if I was the one who went. A few weeks after returning home my father was called to the Hungarian police in Miskolc. He was informed that since he had been born in Slovakia he needed to renew his residency permit every month.

On Sundays I found refuge from the tension and uncertainty that surrounded us. Jewish friends invited me to the Social-Democrat Party clubhouse which had a secret entrance. All the Jewish boys that came there were from assimilated families, and I had not had any previous contact with them. Even though my *peyes* were shortened the boys knew I was from a very traditional family. A person's degree of religious observance could be determined by the neighborhood where he lived. I was not very interested in the club's activities, but I was ready to spend two hours in order to receive a huge sandwich, the likes of which I never saw at home, after the meeting. I stopped going after a few meetings, worried that my parents would discover that I was spending time with "freethinkers".

Winter arrived. Snow piled up in the streets. The authorities assigned work to Jewish boys. Every few days, large notices appeared on houses commanding Jews to report to public buildings to shovel the snow that had accumulated. The overseers were Christian youth, some of whom I knew. Obviously, even those we knew ignored us without any pangs of conscience. In their eyes we were even beneath the Gypsies. Jewish schools were closed in freezing weather since they were not heated.

One Shabbat a rumor spread in the synagogue that Jews who were not Hungarian citizens would be imprisoned, followed by more rumors that were no less alarming. This was part of numerous and varied rumors about assorted edicts, all of which materialized in the end! Meanwhile, Hungarian Christians found a new way to oppress the Jews. From time to time, especially on Friday evenings, groups of rowdy boys would roam through Jewish neighborhoods, breaking house windows. The little quiet we had on Shabbat was also shattered. Until then we used to sit around the fireplace during the long winter evenings. Mother cooked cereal and it was my job to read suspense stories. Now, because of the rampages, stone-throwing and window-breaking, we were forced to turn off the lights in the house to lessen the risk of attack.

Alongside the bad news different accounts were also heard. Although forbidden, people found a way to listen to the BBC that broadcast in Hungarian from London. In synagogue news spread along with exaggerations and analysis. Together with the negative rumors, talk of battles in Russia and Allied advances on the front gave us great hope. The desire to believe that Germany faced defeat lifted our spirits, and Stalin, "the great leader" of the Soviet Union, was called by many the "Savior of the Jews". In many Jewish homes the communist

Internationale was sung as a prayer of liberation from Nazi oppression and a proclamation of the coming of the Messiah.

But nothing actually happened. The Hungarian fascist party grew stronger and the Hungarian people were pleased with the plundering of Jewish property and persecution of the Jews. One evening in 1943 our mother told us that a leader of the Jewish community was organizing the rescue of Jewish children through the Jewish Community Council in Budapest. Word had it that a special train was being organized to take the children to Constantinople in Turkey, and from there to Palestine. This frightened me very much and I did not want to hear about it. My mother however was taken with the idea. She began to run around making arrangements, trying to arrange the large sum of money needed to get my sister Kati and me out of Hungary.

We had no way of knowing whether the information about the train was reliable, but my parents were told one thing: only one child per family would be included in the journey. My parents truly wanted to believe that they would be able to rescue at least one of us. They made superhuman efforts to obtain the needed funds which were far beyond their means.

The money was paid and a few weeks later my mother was notified that there was no room for either of us. My heart filled with resentment against those functionaries who did not bother to refund the precious money scraped together with so much effort!

Meanwhile the frightening events intensified. On one occasion my father reported to the police he was told arrogantly: "Listen Jew, we will soon round up all the foreign citizens and we'll cleanse Hungary of Jews, and then we will have a purified Greater Hungary!"

We lived in fear and apprehension of an unknown future. Most of our conversations revolved around the anticipated downfall of the German-Hungarian forces at the Russian front. Today I know that we did not have the slightest idea of what lay ahead. Hungarian Jewry was complacent and naïve. I was educated to be faithful to the Hungarian flag, and as a child I regarded Hungary as my motherland. In my parents' home there were no expressions of a desire to immigrate to the land of Israel. I heard this only from non-religious children visiting the Mizrachi Zionist Club, and from Christian neighbors who would curse us saying, "Jews, go to Palestine".

My mother hoped that I would be a Torah scholar. How could I tell her about my heretical doubts in the face of persecution and daily harassment by the gentiles? In the winter I would lie huddled beside the stove and daydream. How simple everything would be if I were Christian, if I were one of those boys on the next street…, I would go fearlessly and whenever I wanted to the playground and to public parks, places where Jews were not allowed… I would eat lots of pork meatballs… no one would attack me or push me…

And if I were a Christian, I would certainly not bother Jews! The gentiles are ridiculous: 1,940 years ago they were Jews. Why do they have such a profound hatred of Jews? I did not understand why much of the Christian population was so happy about how things were going. The rise of the Nazis in Europe fascinated them and they did not hide their hatred of Jews. In their eyes the Jews had always been a foreign entity.

"Show us a Jew who works with his hands", our gentile neighbors would challenge us. "You are all richer and smarter. Justice will finally be done in Hungary. The despised Jews will disappear!"

When Jews were attacked on the street, Christian Democrats never showed up to defend them. Even at the Social Democrat youth club, where I went from time to time, I did not hear anything said against the persecution of Jews. When shoveling snow in the streets one day I saw in our midst a man whose head was not covered and his hair parted down the side, a style only adopted by nonreligious Jews. This man had a bicycle shop which was always open on the Shabbat. I had always thought he was a gentile, and here he was among us, shoveling snow with all the Jews! It was interesting to see how the Arrow Cross had identified both religious and secular Jews and separated them out from the community of gentiles.

My mother had once told me that if a Jew was in trouble all he had to do was say *Shema Yisroel* [8], likely the most important prayer in Judaism, and God would rush to help him. As troubles multiplied I would mumble to myself *Shema Yisroel* at every opportunity, but I apparently took advantage of the prayer too many times; God did not rush to help me.

Early one Shabbat morning my father woke us up to tell us that there was talk of foreigners being rounded up for deportation. Surprisingly, my parents did not have Hungarian citizenship. My father had deserted the Czechoslovakian army at the age of 20 and was welcomed with open arms by Hungary, making his home and family here. My sister and I were born in Miskolc. We were all ultra-orthodox *kosher* [9] Hungarians in everyone's eyes until the war, but now we were among the undesirables.

We hurried to pack some food and left the city, heading towards the mountain foothills where my father's cousin lived with his family. We moved through the semi-dark city streets, passing drunks sprawled on the sidewalk here and there, until we reached our relatives. In back of their house were caves and wine cellars owned by Jews, offering plenty of niches where we could hide. Our cousins welcomed us warmly. We spent the Shabbat there, but when our cousin came back from synagogue after evening prayers he advised us to return to our home in the city. To be honest, all of us understood that there was no point in trying to slip away.

The wave of rumors about the fate of Jewish foreigners abounded. To prepare for the danger of deportation awaiting us

---

[8] *Shema Yisroel* - Hear O'Israel, is considered the most important part of the prayer service in Judaism.
[9] *Kosher* – here a slang word for "proper" or "legitimate".

my mother got good winter clothes and sturdy shoes for all of us. She also packed bags of dry food. With all the preparations and constant worry, the arrest came as a complete surprise!

At three in the morning the police arrived at our door. We were woken by loud knocking and given a half hour to pack a bundle for each of us. The neighbors must of heard the police because of the noise they made, but no one stuck his head out. The two policemen hurried us to leave our home quickly. One of my harshest memories is the moment one of them rudely said to my mother, "Lady, leave the key in the door. You won't be coming back here!"

We walked to the central police station. I wanted so badly to run into someone who would tell the rest of our relatives in the city that we had been arrested, but we did not meet a soul. We were not the only prisoners at the police station, but we did not know anyone among the crowd of foreigners.

Registration went on until morning. My mother encouraged us continuously. "God is with us" she repeated, "We have always been righteous and kept his commandments and he will not desert us now".

I kept quiet. I recalled my small sins over the past two years, all the non-kosher sandwiches I had eaten, the joy I felt when my aunt "evened" my *peyes*…I was guilt stricken but had hopes that my mother's good relations with the Holy One on High would help me as well; after all, I had learned in the *Cheder* that Sodom was not destroyed thanks to one righteous person.

We were taken to the train station in the morning and told to get on the train with the regular passengers. We were warned not to talk to them but the warning was unnecessary, the other passengers stayed away. The train traveled in the direction of Budapest. The children and youngsters were engrossed in the trip itself. I had been to Budapest only once before, in 1938, when I was ten years old. I was very impressed and bragged to my friends about my adventures in the beautiful big city.

My father was a natural actor. He sat silently beside me,

holding my hand in his, and giving me an encouraging squeeze from time to time. He told me not to worry, and described life in Czechoslovakia, since we would be deported there from Budapest… Of course no one knew then that there were no more Jews in Czechoslovakia; they had all been deported to concentration camps. Even though Jewish refugees from Poland had reached our city, the complacency of Hungarian Jews was inexplicable. They found it convenient to believe that nothing would happen to them.

We reached Budapest. We got off the train and walked close to each other without looking around. We were put on trucks and driven through the busy city. The passersby did not even look our way. We reached a huge gloomy building with a small sign: Police. The police station was only used to round up foreign nationals before they were deported. The place hummed with the noise of people of various origins, mostly Jews. I began to think that my father was right and that the situation was not so bad; that in my father's birthplace, Czechoslovakia, the situation would no doubt be different…

Registration was exhausting, hours during which we did not receive any food. At the end of the process the women were separated from the men. This was the last time I saw my mother.

It was very crowded in the large hall where my father and I ended up. We were commanded to sit in rows, each of us leaning his head on his bundle. We remained in this position the entire day. To reach the toilet we had to wait in a very long line. The next day we were told that anyone who wanted kosher food or a personal package had to give the address of his relatives in Budapest, and would be allowed to receive food from them. Like the others, we gave the address of our relatives in the city.

Very few people came to visit. We understood that the Jews were afraid. No one from our family came but we kept our disappointment to ourselves. Several times we received food from the Joint, the Jewish relief organization. Most of the time we were fed well by the authorities. The problem was not food but the crowded conditions. The nights were unbearable. We slept cramped together, suffering headaches from the heat and strong odors. A man near us began to show too much interest in my welfare. He felt my forehead and told my father I had a fever. I woke up several times during the night, feeling him paw me. He said he was concerned about me. I felt him put his hand under my shirt. I turned to him and told him quietly to stop at once or I would wake my father. He was so concerned about me that he crawled away to find another place to sleep. I was very proud of my father's strong appearance and broad shoulders. I thought the man did not want a confrontation with him. The next morning my father asked me where that nice man went. I kept quiet and said nothing.

Sárvár Camp

After two weeks we were taken to Sárvár Camp in western Hungary, an area where most of the population was Swabian, Hungarians of German origin. The place was expansive, filled with old buildings and barracks. The people were Jews from different countries. We befriended just a few. We did not understand why we had been separated from my mother and sister as there were also women here. We still believed that we were being deported to our countries of origin, in our case Czechoslovakia.

The regime at Sárvár Camp was not strict. The Hungarian policemen were rude and arrogant. They were the notorious peasant police and their job was to guard the camp periphery.

Their outfit resembled an army uniform, except that they wore a sort of black round hat with a feather on the side. Soup was distributed once a day and in the evening we received a thick slice of bread and sausage seasoned with lots of garlic. Rumor had it that the sausage was made of horse meat, but this made no difference to us. At that point in our life we were happy to get an additional slice of sausage from Jews in the camp who did not eat it, either because they were keeping *kosher* or had money to buy other food.

My father ran out of cigarettes after a while and was very miserable. Thanks to an idea I had, my father soon had more than enough cigarettes. At the bottom of our knapsack I found a large package of powder (RAZOL) used for shaving by religious Jews. My father sat outside the barracks while I prepared a cream from the shaving powder and was soon giving him a shave. Immediately a line of curious onlookers was formed of those ready to pay for the same service. I finished the supply of powder within three days, but managed to amass enough money to supply my father with cigarettes for a long time.

I wandered around the camp all day long, in and out of the living quarters, looking for something to do. I gathered a lot of news. There was talk of breaking out of the camp. I heard that there was contact with people on the outside and that there were gentiles ready to help Jews, for large sums of money. I do not know if there were any escapes; we were counted every day before the food was distributed.

One phenomenon especially sparked my interest. A man would show up once in a while with a stool on which he stood, giving fiery speeches about the need to maintain quiet and order. "Soon we will all be going to work in Germany. We will all have better lives when we are resettled", he would say. Most of us listened to his reassuring words; we desperately wanted to believe that our situation would get better.

From time to time we received postcards from my mother

and sister, notifying us that "We are fine and healthy". The postal mark was unclear. We had no idea where they were and we had no way of getting in touch with them.

As time passed I got to know some of the other camp inhabitants. There were only a few boys my age, but we did not become friends. I still covered my head with a cap which I did not remove, because walking around bareheaded, without my *kippah* (skullcap), made me uncomfortable. As I wandered around the camp I found people lying on beds with nothing to do most of the day. Here and there a crowd would gather around various singers and musicians who struggled to breathe life into the dismal environment. I particularly remember a delightful young man who entertained the crowd with clowning acts and card tricks. He fooled everyone with cards. Policemen from the camp staff would sometimes join the crowd of onlookers. Everyone would make room for them and stand apart from them. Once I heard a policeman say that he could not stand the smell of Jews…The policemen tried to guess which cards were hidden, and of course failed. That is why the poor guy got slapped by the police at the end of his show. They could not endure the burning insult that a Jew could beat them. "Give in to them, let the police win", the Jewish onlookers urged him. But he stood his ground. That was his small victory over the *goyim (Gentiles)*.

My father never came to the performances with me. My reports were enough for him. I rejoiced every time I coaxed a smile out of him. He would often sigh and say that instead of him taking care of me, I was taking care of him. See, I even bought him cigarettes…

My first shock at the camp occurred when I visited the women's barracks. I went there on the excuse that I was looking for a certain boy. What my eyes saw stunned me. Actually, I frequently saw couples meet during the daylight hours and go for a walk together, but here, in the barracks, for the first time in my life I saw couples laying together naked in bed making love in broad daylight! The women in the nearby beds sang war songs popular at the time, such as "We have one day left in the world". It was as if my feet were stuck to the ground. I could not move and I could not leave. I looked around, and everywhere saw couples laying together, getting drunk, and singing. I thought to myself that maybe their end of the world had really arrived.

I did not tell my father about this; I did not dare tell him that I had been in the women's barracks. The idleness and limited amount of food had a severe effect on my father, which included long periods of silence between us. During the nightly distribution of sausage I noticed that he would intentionally eat slowly, and when he saw that I had finished my portion he would push his piece towards me, claiming that his portion had been bigger and that he was already full. In response, I would pat my stomach, as if it were full, and I always managed to convince him that I was full and could not eat any more.

There was no registration process at Camp Sárvár. Most of the inmates, mainly the younger ones, were born in Hungary to parents who had come from various countries, mainly from Romania, Poland, and Czechoslovakia. They were all Jews, and therefore I did not believe the rumor that we would all be sent back to our countries of origin.

How long were we at the camp? We did not count the days or the weeks. Once I heard that prisoners carved a notch each day to mark the passing of time, but I did not have anything on which to mark grooves or anything with which to carve them. I knew that I had to store everything in my memory. Nonetheless, I estimated that we were at Camp Sárvár for two months. And then, one spring morning, we were commanded to line up according to our country of origin. We waited with hearts filled with fear about what was to come. Tables and chairs were brought out to the open square. Documents and registration forms were piled on each table. Registration was carried out by police officers, civil servants, and two German officers. We knew very well that the Germans had a military pact with the Hungarians, and we managed to guess that the registration was for "resettlement". Whoever still entertained the notion of being sent back to the countries of origins was disillusioned.

I recalled all the speeches in camp, meant to keep things calm with talk of the German war effort. They explained that the Germans needed foreign workers, and that, "It's not so terrible to go work in Germany. No one would harm us. What could be worse than this place?"

And truthfully, what could be worse than this, a place with no medical care for the many sick people?... My thoughts were interrupted when the first names in the lineup were called. Four people were registered quietly and returned to the orderly lines. Suddenly an uproar broke out. A person got out of line before his name was called. The entire camp had seen this person before. We did not know if he was really crazy or only pretending. He used to say that the mentally ill would not be deported. He claimed that if they saw that he was crazy, the most they would do would be to hospitalize him in Hungary. We were accustomed to seeing him go on a rampage and create a commotion in every lineup. The Hungarian overseers did not do anything to him, only made fun of him.

However, this time everything became absolutely still. The man went up to the table. We did not hear what he said, but from his previous outbursts we knew that he wanted to be imprisoned in a Hungarian mental hospital. We saw the Hungarian officers confer in secret with the two German officers present, apparently telling them about the man.

We saw the German officers get up from their places immediately. For the first time in my life I saw their uniforms in all their glory; up until now I had only seen pictures in newspapers. The uniform included shiny boots, Nazi insignia on the sleeve, a visored hat with a skull embroidered in silver thread, and white gloves. One of the German officers took a small step toward the "crazy Jew". The man was instantly sprawled on the ground, bleeding. The German remained standing, one foot in its shiny boot on the man's stomach, as if he were stepping on an insect on the floor. The Jew got up and ran away limping and bleeding. His shouts were heard throughout the entire field. The German sat down peacefully at the table, as if nothing had happened.

The policemen announced that registration would continue the next day. We dispersed. Throughout the evening we were busy interpreting the event. Some took comfort in the fact that the crazy person was guilty of the chaos: "Who asked him to go on a rampage", they asked. Even then, very few thought that the Germans were monsters. And how could we explain their behavior at the lineup? It was convenient to believe that the Germans loved order, and that they only wanted to show us what discipline meant. After all, the person had dared to leave his place in line and to approach the table without being called!

The following days were relatively quiet. Again the regular speakers with their stools appeared, and again we heard reassuring words. "If the registration could be completed quietly then we would all go to work in a factory in Germany, receive food rations like all the German people, and certainly be able to correspond with our families from whom we had been separated".

Rumor followed rumor: "registration was stopped because of the people's lack of discipline…soon the trains ordered for us would arrive…assignment to factories would be done in Germany". Many people got on the sick list, complaining of exhaustion and various illnesses after a rumor started that people not fit for work because of advanced age would be left in camp…

When the unrest from the uncertainty grew, Hungarian officers suddenly visited the camp to calm the worriers, promising that nothing bad would happen to them.

It was business as usual along the camp fences, with large amounts of money changing hands. Wide-eyed I would watch the scene. How did people have so much money and jewelry? The price of food along the fences skyrocketed. I saw a Jew sell a gold watch for a loaf of bread and a sausage. People with means stored enough food to last them until they reached Germany. One day, while standing beside the fence, I heard Christian boys saying that they had seen a long line of freight trains with barbed wire around the openings. People heard this and assumed that the freight trains were for the camp inmates' belongings. We would certainly be traveling in passenger trains, like the ones in which we had arrived – it seemed to them completely logical.

The older Jews would repeat the standard saying: "Everything is in the hands of the One above, good Jews, don't worry, have faith in our God!" I did not need to be convinced. I was raised by my religious mother. I knew that everything would be all right; I just did not understand how. And why did they need so many freight cars? We did not have a lot of belongings; each of us had left the house with only one bundle. I wanted to believe the reassurances, but conflicting thoughts raced through my mind. I heard the rascals by the fence saying that there were no passenger trains in the entire area; that the freight cars were meant for transporting Jews from Sárvár to Germany. I tried to deceive myself into thinking that this was only a dream, that I would wake up and find myself at home in Miskolc. I pledged to go to prayers, morning and evening, to do all my homework, to confess to my mother about the pork sandwiches, but please, God, do something, let us return and be reunited at home.

I closed my eyes and muttered a thousand oaths and promises, repeated *Shema Yisroel* fervently several times a day, and began to believe that my prayers would help us. I even accepted the hunger with understanding. I would cover my head with the blanket and count the items on a holiday menu, and it always worked. Before going to sleep I would press my stomach to stop the loud rumblings in my body, and this is how I would fall asleep. However, waking up was always difficult since my stomach was still empty. My father and I, like most of the camp inmates, did not have enough money to buy food at the fence. My father closely guarded a white bag containing dried noodles which my mother had prepared for the journey. Every morning he took out a spoonful of noodles and boiled them in water. When the noodles were soft we divided the delicacy between us. First we drank the liquid, then we fished the noodles, one by one, so the meal would last longer.

One morning we awoke to the sound of the loudspeakers blasting throughout the entire camp: "Get in the lineup immediately together with your belongings".

I knew it was coming. I can't say I was surprised. I regretted one thing: why didn't they wait until after distribution of the daily sausage?

There was utter confusion. All our illusions were shattered. If everyone was reporting to the lineup, that was a sign that everyone was leaving the camp. And what about the stories that only the fit would be sent? The little scamp by the fence and I both knew the truth about the freight cars with the barbed wire around the openings. Deep inside I had not believed the reassuring assessments of those who had given speeches. I knew that it was all a deception. Nevertheless, I found some satisfaction when I saw one of them walking with a bent head, bundle in hand like everyone else, silent, no longer making speeches...Had they believed their own speeches? Another thought I had - all the times I had recited *Shema Yisroel* had been for nothing.

The procession began to walk toward the train station. We had very few possessions. My father in his wisdom had left the down comforter behind in the barracks and wrapped our few belongings in a regular blanket. I did not dare ask why he had left the down comforter. Along the way I wondered why they did not separate out those fit for work. And what would they do with the sick and elderly? Would they separate them when they put us on the train?

We got to the railroad tracks, exhausted. I was surprised to see the platform bustling with people; thousands of curious individuals came from the surrounding area to witness the deportation of the Jews. I could not count all the cars waiting along the station because of the crowd of onlookers.

Dozens of Hungarian policemen formed a human chain to separate us from the inquisitive onlookers. The overcrowding was terrible. Heat, hunger, and fear paralyzed me. I did not say a word. I held onto my father's hand tightly so I would not get lost in the confusion. We moved forward slowly and stood beside the cars. German soldiers waited for a signal to open the doors. Suddenly I saw large carts being pushed by workers. The carts were piled with loaves of fresh bread; the aroma reached me and tickled my nostrils.

The shouts for order were terrible vulgar. In addition to the Hungarian police, there was a long line of German soldiers alongside the cars. The Hungarian citizens were distanced, voicing their disappointment that they could not see the splendid sight of the Jews rounded up to be deported...They came joyfully to bid us farewell with a smile.

The first cars arrived. The doors were opened and the Jews streamed in. Every car was closed and locked. German SS staff and Hungarian policemen approached our group. "Look," I said to my father, "there is no selection for work! The old, sick, crippled, and lame are loaded on to the cars with everyone else."

My father asked me to stick close to him. We were lucky not to have excess baggage; those who had many bundles were hustled with rifle butts and whips to move faster. Our group was loaded very quickly. We had no time to think about what we should do. We were already being pushed in, and about one hundred fresh loaves of bread were thrown into the car.

Everyone grabbed one. I was nimble and managed to get us the two loaves we were due. The journey began.

No one knew exactly how long we were en route. The estimate was that we traveled for a week. Suddenly the train stopped and the doors opened.

2.

Auschwitz-Birkenau

My father and I got off without any help. We found ourselves standing in a huge square. At the center of the square was a large group of soldiers, some in black uniforms with the skull decorating the hat visor. Not a sound escaped us. Many strong-looking young men ran around the train dressed in striped clothing and striped caps. Numbers and a red cloth triangle were sewn on their prisoner clothes. There were also other identifying signs on some prisoners, usually in black, which I did not yet understand.

Today I know: They were the overseers, the *kapos* [10], prisoners assigned by the SS to oversee the other prisoners. They had rubber sticks hanging from their hands, and they used them to hurry the prisoners along. Their job was to drag out the elderly who could not get off on their own and to remove the corpses. Bodies were piled up along the train. I did not know if they were unconscious or dead. I heard people in the distance shouting, looking for their relatives. Their voices were cut off by the insistent beating. It was the first time I heard the shouts ordering us to hurry: "*los eintreten*" (go fast

---

[10] *Kapo* - a prisoner in a Nazi concentration camp assigned by the SS guards to supervise forced labor or carry out administrative tasks. Part of the SS prisoner functionary system.

to be counted). Anyone who did not understand was pushed brutally by the *kapos*.

The Selection

The lines formed slowly. It seemed that everyone was looking for someone. Most of the deportees quickly understood that it was best to be silent. The beatings on shoulders and heads were cruel in their precision. My father asked that I stay in line, not look around and turn my back to the overseers so as not to be noticed. That's how I escaped pointless beatings. Finally the lines formed to the *kapos'* satisfaction. People were counted several times, until the total number, including the corpses nearby that were taken off the train, matched the number of passengers put on the cars. We were moved along from there.

In the distance I saw a group of prisoners piling our bundles in a heap. I understood that no one's personal possessions would be returned. A huge field stretched out in front of us, with a large group of German soldiers standing opposite us. Far away, strange frightening barbed wire fences with watchtowers rising up over the horizon could be seen.

The large group moved forward very slowly. From where we were we could not see what was happening in front. The *kapos* moved through the lines, telling us to take off our coats and shirts and get into one line. My father whispered to me to stretch myself tall, stand very straight, and throw out my chest, so that I would look bigger and stronger than my age. He also told me to stand right in back of him.

I did not know the reason for the selection but I could easily see that all the sick and the elderly, the women and the small children, were sent to the left, and the adults and youth, fit for hard labor, were sent to the right. Undoubtedly it would be better to be on the right.

The selection went very fast. When we reached the front of the area I saw the SS officer responsible for the selection. I learned later that he was the infamous Dr. Josef Mengele. He wore a black sharply pressed uniform and had glasses. We stood motionless. Not a sound escaped us. I could now see from close up the man pointing right or left by tilting the officer's club he was holding. Sometimes the line stopped. The officer spat out a few words, with a strange smile on his face as he used his stick to lift the sunken chin of a young woman or used it to poke her breast.

My father did not dare to turn around to give me advice, but as we quickly learned, everything was random. I saw boys my age being sent to the left with the aged and weak, and I knew that I did not want to be among them. It was my father's turn. Since he had broad shoulders he was quickly sent to the right. Three people were between us. I felt unsure of myself but I took his advice. I held my head high and threw out my chest, and I succeeded! I passed in front of the SS officer and his stick pointed "right"!

Now we were taken to another field. Many among us continued to look dumbfounded, seeking out relatives with their eyes. People who knew us nodded their heads at our luck on remaining together, even though in their opinion my physical shape was far from satisfactory. I was not angry at them; everyone looked out for himself. Anyway, I didn't let them spoil my joy in being with my father.

In the distance I could see that the elderly, the women and the children were being loaded onto trucks, but at the time we did not yet realize their destination. *Kapos* appeared immediately, explaining in various languages that we needed to be obedient. We are going to the showers now, they said, and we would get new striped clothes, like they themselves were wearing. After another lineup the *kapos* began their reassuring speeches: "You won't need the possessions you left beside the train. Don't worry, all your needs will be met here". And also, "Anyone who has anything valuable must place it on the blanket spread out here. After the shower, everyone will be x-rayed. Anyone found to possess anything of value will be sent to the trucks you saw over there".

I was amazed to see the amount of jewelry piled on the blanket. My father whispered to me to throw my wristwatch on the blanket. "It's broken anyway. Some day you will get another one".

I emptied my pockets of "souvenirs" I had kept until now: a favorite small penknife and some pictures from home. The line began to move forward on an unpaved path. The large man walking beside me seemed familiar. All at once I recognized him: he was the irritating Jew who had sat beside us in the freight car from Hungary, covering his head with his coat and chewing on a garlic salami during the ride. Now the same person turned to me and offered a candy. I recalled the salami, the smell of garlic, and the hunger during the trip, and I scornfully turned down the candy.

We reached an enormous camp. There was considerable activity around the large barracks. We were ordered into the central building, told to undress, and to tie our shoes onto our hands with the shoelaces. At this point I understood that there was no reason to hide anything in our pockets, and I was happy that I had thrown everything onto the pile.

Before entering the showers we were all checked again, and again rushed with shouts to hurry. The *kapos* encircled us, holding rubber clubs, and any unnecessary movement led to blows. We were led to a huge hall and sat naked on benches waiting our turn for the barbers. Dozens of electric cords for razors hung from the ceiling. The "haircut" was quick. After our heads were shaved, we spread our legs and lifted our arms; all our body hair was shaved off, and not gently.

Next to the barber hall were the latrine pits. For the first time, I relieved myself while stooping. The *kapos* passed by us, "accidentally" shoving someone here and there. I caught on that I should not look at them. For no reason I got pushed and slapped. It was a good thing my father was not nearby to see the treatment I got. I sensed that the day would come when I would be alone and would need to face my problems on my own.

We were told that after the shower we would go back to the lineup and get our food ration. The water in the shower was hot but the soap had no suds and we felt as if we were washing ourselves with sandpaper. After the shower we moved towards the clothes storehouse. Two men stood with pails of disinfectant in the passage. They dipped the brush in the pail and smeared the solution between our outspread legs and our armpits. At first it felt pleasant and cool, but then changed to a burning sensation. No one dared complain. Everyone feared the rubber clubs. I received a hat, a jacket, pants, and long underwear. We were warned harshly that the clothes were the property of the German Reich; we were to take good care of them. No one would get anything else. Luckily I was given clothes my size.

I was glad the "disinfection" stage was over. We waited in the square for the others to finish. I searched for my father among those in the square. I went all around, pulling the sleeve of anyone who looked like him. When I found him, I was amazed at how he had changed. His pants were too short, and the barber had left half his moustache, out of carelessness or deliberate cruelty. My father complained that he had also been cut in the other places they had shaved him.

During the two hours we stood and waited we learned details about the life that awaited us. The name of the place was "Auschwitz-Birkenau". All the people sent to the left during the selection were no longer alive. The crematoria in the four corners of the camp worked day and night. The *kapos* told us that all the sick, the elderly, the children, and all others unfit for labor were put to death in the gas chambers, and taken to the crematoria in Birkenau.

I did not tell my father of the horrors I heard. With feigned calm I listened to his explanation, "Calm down, Moshe-Yankel, everything will be all right. Look, we are alive! That is where they are burning the clothes we didn't need that we left in a pile". I was silent. What could I say? I looked around. The sun was about to set. The sky was gray. Only in the four corners of the camp was the sky lit with a red glow. Clouds of smoke sank from time to time, and a smell spread through the field, similar to the smell of the scorched flesh of chickens when my mother would make them kosher after plucking.

We sat in silence, each keeping to himself. It seemed to me that years had gone by since we had left Hungary. I continued to think about the people who had died and were no longer here, that for them it was all over; but for us, the living, certainly better times awaited us.

"The healthy and strong ones among us will be sent to labor camps", people whispered to each other. I peeked at my father, a healthy man! And me? If only I were a little heavier my chances of being sent to work would be greater. I recalled all the glasses of milk I had refused to drink as a child. I nodded off while crouching. It was pleasant to dream, even about milk that I once hated. Except that the stench of Auschwitz was terrifying. People told me that only at dusk was the stench this strong. The wind picked up, gathering wisps of smoke with the sparks. "In the morning it will be fresh and clean", they promised.

The last of the group arrived and an uproar broke out on the field. "*Juden entreten*" (Jews, roll call),the *kapos* hollered. Again we all got into groups of five, the standard German formation. Here and there cries of pain were heard from those beaten with the clubs to hurry them. I promised my father to be quick in order to avoid unnecessary blows. We began to walk.

Day was ending as we arrived at the numbered barracks, long wooden huts sided with tarpaper. The distance between them was about 100 meters. Every barrack, I learned after roll call, housed one thousand men. I picked up from rumors that the camp was called the "*Tzigoiner Lager*" (Gypsy Camp), and that next to us there was also camp A, and also camp B - names I understood the next morning.

We milled around the area. *Kapos* suddenly appeared together with prisoners similar to us, except that their clothes were better. They were the "functionaries", prisoners assigned by the SS to carry out administrative tasks. They held up blankets with pieces of bread piled on them. This was the first food we received since getting off the train. Later I learned that: no roll call, no food. A large group of thuggish *kapos* stood by the entrance to the barracks. As we entered, each of us got a piece of bread and a shove.

I saw our living quarters for the first time. They were exactly like all the other barracks I would experience after Auschwitz-Birkenau. The barrack was divided in two. Along the walls on each side were three tiers of wooden bunks. In the center, the entire length of the barrack, ran a brick structure about a meter wide. I found out that this was once a furnace for heating horse stables, when the Poles still had cavalry. Guards stood along the length of the structure with clubs in their hands, hurrying us along to the back of the barrack and on to the bunks. I ate my bread quickly so my hands would be free to climb to up the top bunk. Actually, I did not know where it was better to sleep, but I preferred climbing up to where some light entered the barrack. I lay down on the bunk with difficulty. The shouts to hurry grew louder. There were still people outside and the *kapos* kept pushing more and more people onto the bunks. It was very crowded. I could not move. I had to remain in my original position without being able to turn over. The shouting continued for a long time. People shouted about the bread that was snatched from their hands, and I was happy that I had eaten mine.

When the noise lessened the Block functionaries[11] announced that no one was allowed to leave until morning, not even to go to the latrine. The night was intolerable. I slept a few hours, thanks to my luck getting a top bunk. From the shouts it appeared that many could not hold their bladder all night, urinating as they lay on the bunk, dripping on those below.

The next morning we got up before daybreak. We were hustled out of the barracks and made to stand in the square between them. Those in the other barracks were also outdoors. The Blockmasters[12] warned us not to stray. We remained standing like that, crowded, until the sun came out. After much searching, I found my father. We looked at each other and breathed a sigh of relief that we were together again.

The lineup began, and the count went on forever. We were weak from hunger and thirst but the *kapos* announced that the lineup would not end until the numbers matched their lists. Finally the last count was exact, and the number was recorded by a man, the *shreiber* (registrar clerk), wearing a prison uniform like us, but smoothly ironed. Actually, all the workers and those with jobs looked to me well-fed and shaved, as if they came from a different world.

Now we were free to wash up. I saw the clever camp latrine for the first time: a big building with a urinal channel running along the wall. In the center were two low walls. The area between the two walls formed another channel, and a long wooden rod hung balanced above. To use the latrine we had to pull our pants down to the floor and hold onto the rod with two hands. Otherwise we could not sit on the edge of the wall without risking falling into the channel.

---

[11] The prisoner functionary system was comprised of prisoners who supervised or carried out administrative functions. For further information see the glossary.
[12] Blockmaster - block or barrack leader.

It was a grotesque sight. As if that were not enough, there were people who took advantage of the helplessness of someone sitting on the latrine to go through the pockets of his dangling pants. Here and there a piece of bread, carefully saved, could be found. Again I learned that the portion of bread should be eaten immediately to thwart the bread thieves. I proudly told my father how experienced I was becoming.

We were rushed back to the square where the lineup and count had taken place. A group of SS soldiers suddenly appeared before us. The clerks, who were also prisoners, and all the Blockmasters, lined up to prevent us from approaching the tables in the center of the square. Pages of lists with numbers were on the tables. From time to time men who looked stronger than the rest were taken out of the group, brought to the table, and a number from the list was tattooed on their left arm. The selection went on until the afternoon hours. No one knew if there was an advantage to getting a number. My father also had a number tattooed on his arm. After those with numbers were separated from the group I realized that I had been separated from him. Then I realized that those with numbers were being taken to the neighboring camp. Together with the shock of being separated, it dawned on me that those remaining with me were either young like me or older than my father.

I didn't have much time to ponder this. We were quickly hustled into the barrack, with a small piece of bread like yesterday. Two days had gone by and I still did not know what my fate would be. One evening new people were added, those remaining from a selection in a nearby barrack, and they also had no tattoo on their arm. The next day was different: no morning lineup. At noon a small group of kitchen workers showed up. They brought two wooden barrels, each one hanging from a pole. The poles were carried on the shoulders of the workers. Someone in our midst still had enough of a sense of humor to say in juicy Yiddish[13]: "Here come the spies

---

[13] Yiddish — a Germanic language and the language of central and eastern

to spy out the land, carrying on their shoulders the fruits of the good land…", a passage from the Bible describing the spies dispatched by Moses to scout out the land of Canaan.

The barrels were put down beside the barrack, and the aroma of the frightening concoction drove us wild. Faint from hunger we crowded around the barrels. I could feel how my feet no longer touched the ground as I was carried in the air by the crowd. The Blockmasters hurried to bring order. The *blockälteste* [14] (Block elder) appeared with a ladle, along with other workers carrying tin plates of every size and shape. Loud arguments broke out as the food was distributed. I saw how the stronger ones managed to get in line twice, grabbing empty plates and getting more soup. The hunger gnawing inside me propelled me to push ahead. If I didn't, I knew I would not get any food, and I had to look out for myself. I succeeded in making it up to the servers, received my portion, and swallowed it in big gulps without looking to see what it contained. In a split-second someone grabbed my empty plate and licked it on all sides.

The next day there was morning lineup. We were instructed to stay in the vicinity of the barrack because the noontime soup would be distributed early. I mingled with the other thousand people and listened to the countless explanations of every word that came out of the mouths of those with jobs. These included for example: "They are just waiting for the place to fill up with people from additional transports and then we'll be sent to the place where they send those unable to work; who knows where that is".

Several SS officers appeared. For the next few hours they had to be entertained. The officers approached those in the back of the lineup, grabbed two people who looked relatively strong, pulled them to the front and asked them why they

---

European Jews.

[14] *Blockälteste* (block elder) – a prisoner functionary whose duties were to maintain order and discipline in the block, to distribute food and keep records of the prisoners. The block elders had almost unlimited power over the prisoners.

were quarreling during the lineup, which had actually been conducted in total silence. The two said they did not know each other and that they were not quarreling. The SS officer pushed them against each other and ordered one of them: "Hit him! I saw how he was hitting you during the lineup!"

One of them slapped the other just to obey the command. But the SS officer was not satisfied. "Like this! Hit him harder, like this!", he said as he hit the other one. "If you don't hit like this, I'll teach you how!"

Given no choice they began to hit each other. The officer did not let them stop until they were both on the ground bleeding. Only then was he satisfied with the show, and left us muttering, "Look how those Jews kill each other!"

The show was repeated daily, and the Germans enjoyed it anew each time.

The Bottom Bunk

Additional transports arrived. Many people were added to our barrack and the place overflowed. I became friendly with two new boys my age, and we conversed in Yiddish. They had also survived the selection, a few days before me, and they knew more than me about what was happening. I heard from them that all those who remained here without a tattooed number would end up being exterminated. I took their advice to join them in sleeping on the bottom bunk. That way we could talk without being bothered. One of them explained to me that if they came to take us away in the middle of the night, all we needed to do was to loosen two or three boards and squeeze through the opening to get out of the barrack.

SS men with dogs came at night, turned on all the lights, and very quickly began to empty the barrack of all inhabitants. Trucks were waiting outside. The shouts and pleas were of no use; truck after truck was loaded with Jews. My two bunkmates managed to loosen the lower boards of the barrack wall. Even though the boards were loose, we continued to lie on the bunk. We were afraid of the dogs running around and sniffing everything. I don't know how my mates thought we could make it out through the temporary opening we had made during the day. No one could hear anything because of the awful chaos. The workers whipped people with their clubs. I could not understand their enthusiasm in hitting the prisoners: they themselves were prisoners! Apparently the SS were in a big rush and we were lucky they did not check all the lower bunks carefully, perhaps because of the awful stench that arose from there. In any case, we were not discovered.

The trucks left without us. Outside things calmed down, as if nothing had happened. I dozed off a bit, wondering how we would get our portion of bread: if there were no people in the barrack, there was no roll call – no roll call, no bread!

At daybreak a new group appeared in the barrack. We realized that we had survived. The new ones looked no better than the previous group. We blended into the crowd. They did not know each other anyway. Our only fear was that the workers would recognize one of us during the bread distribution. By now I was also well-trained in soup distribution. I knew enough to be ready when the barrel-carriers showed up so I could be among the first in line when they reached us.

Despite the surprises and unexpected incidents that occurred daily, life had a certain routine. The lines formed as usual, the workers were the same people as yesterday, only the prisoners were new. How could I explain to the newcomers that it would be in their interest to keep things orderly because, if not, food distribution would not go smoothly? The adults wouldn't listen to a boy like me and I didn't dare tell them that I was a "veteran" here.

Regrettably, food distribution was disrupted. At the front of the line arguments broke out and the Blockmaster shouted in amusement "*Verfluchte Juden*" (Damned Jews). "If there is no order here, no one will eat!"

Even though they were prisoners like us, the behavior of the workers and functionaries was crueler than that of the SS, perhaps because they wanted to curry favor in the eyes of the German officers. Throughout the entire day, especially during food distribution, we were at their mercy. We were all Jewish prisoners and the barrack *kapos* were Gypsies. I concluded that Gypsies were preferable to Jews.

I looked into the soup barrels and tried to guess what would happen now. Surely they wouldn't drag them back when they were half-full…therefore, they would surely portion out the contents. Based on what I had received the past two days I calculated that they contained at least 400 liters. So today I should be getting an especially full bowl.

Some SS men drew near and asked the *kapos* what the uproar was all about and why they were not distributing the soup. The *kapos* pointed at us, saying that the Jews were creating confusion and not maintaining order.

"*Mach dos schnell*" (do it fast) the SS officers shouted, and they pushed over the barrels.

The people instantly lunged at the spilt soup. Everyone was pushing and shoving, so I got far away to avoid being trampled. The SS officers looked on with contempt and scorn at the mass of people on their hands and knees scooping up with their hands the soup that had not been absorbed into the ground. Within minutes there was no trace of soup; the ground had been licked clean.

"Accursed Jews, from now on, you will know how to be orderly", the SS officers shouted as they left.

Normally, very few volunteered to return the barrels. They

would crawl inside the barrel and scrape the sides for every drop of soup. Today, there were many volunteers because there was more than the usual amount of soup clinging to the sides after it was deliberately spilled.

In the evening, during bread distribution, my partners from last night and I stayed together. They told me there was still a chance to get into a work group. They heard that sometimes those without numbers were also called to work. I began to mull over the idea, to imagine it.

That night I thought about my father for the first time. Where was he, what was his fate? I felt pangs of guilt, how could the hunger distance all of my family from my heart? Yes, the hunger oppressed me greatly. All day long I dwelled on the thought that perhaps that night I would get a bigger piece of bread. At that point I was unaware that the *kapos* routinely made the portions smaller, and traded with the extra bread.

The next afternoon, when we stood as usual between the barracks, the sky suddenly became cloudy and torrential rain came down on us. We were not allowed to go into the barrack, because it might disrupt the nightly bread distribution. We stood there dripping wet as the rain continued to fall. Suddenly there was a break, and a kind of black cloud sank onto the field, covering it with a distinct stench. The furnaces of Auschwitz were operating at full speed. We choked and felt nauseated. People began to vomit. I knew from experience that I needed to restrain myself, since I had nothing to vomit out.

I stood with my two friends. There was no point talking about the furnaces. We tried to breathe through the heavy stench that surrounded us. Were we becoming indifferent to everything? We were standing there thinking of nothing more than the bread we would get this evening, as humans were going up in smoke through the chimneys!

The day grew dark. Our wet clothes were dripping. Who knows how many people would become sick tonight; most of us were already coughing. Finally, the blankets carrying the bread arrived. At least we got our portion immediately upon entering the barrack. I didn't bother checking if today's portion was larger or smaller than yesterday's. The taste of bread in my mouth was almost like something from the Garden of Eden. I alternated between tearing into it and sniffing the crust, doubling my enjoyment. My neighbor couldn't understand the purpose of smelling it. I wasn't going to give up my double enjoyment. At home I also had the habit of inhaling the scent of bread crust.

It was impossible to sleep at night. It seemed as if everyone in the barrack was groaning and coughing. At midnight the Block workers got out of their beds, turned on the light, and asked: "who doesn't feel well?" The naïve ones who responded got clubbed indiscriminately: "I'll cure you with this! There is no better medicine than a beating!"

Quiet returned to the barrack. As my clothes began to dry out I began to feel itching all over my body. I could not scratch myself because I could not roll over in the bunk. From time to time I heard a shout as someone was pushed out of the bunk and fell to the floor. I envied him; at least now he could scratch himself.

In the morning, when I left the barrack, I heard the Block workers commenting ironically that, "you are finally in shape for the next transport. That will cure your cough!"

The sun was shining and our clothes dried out. We were so weakened that I forgot about the nasty night. I looked around and tried to think of the sunshine and the blue sky, and tried to ignore the smoke rising from the chimneys. Who knows, maybe it was all a dream? Look, the sun is in the sky, only the horizon is out of sight, and there is not even one tree to be seen, or one bird: opposite me are black rotting barracks. Everything is gray-black. There are no other colors on the planet of Auschwitz.

Buttons in my Soup

Along the road separating camps A, B, and C, the SS soldiers walk with their dogs. Their uniforms are black and their boots are shiny. What proud descendants of Goethe and Schiller... and the German language rich with expressions we heard from their progeny: "*Dreckige Juden*" (Dirty Jews), "**dreck zak**" (shitbag) and more. And these people believed that they were "members of the superior race!" But it was better to put these thoughts aside and quickly learn the rules - Do not look into the eye of a *kapo*, and never make eye contact with an SS soldier; Keep your head bent, your eyes to the ground, and stand at attention. Between roll calls I milled around among people. Maybe I would overhear something new. I heard talk in a mixture of languages, a veritable Tower of Babel. Everyone was talking about their dreams and fantasies, not listening to anyone else. Only the barrels of food put a stop to the sighing and the stories. All eyes focused on the food when it arrived. Each day I discovered anew that I did not have enough strength to push to the head of the line, and perhaps I counted on my good luck. Look, I got a bowl of soup and it was thick soup... at the bottom of the bowl I found two buttons, and the soup itself was thin and tasteless. There was no way of knowing its contents. And the buttons? I received a reasonable explanation: every day the freight cars arriving in Auschwitz are cleaned out, and the scraps of food and other "findings" are thrown into the soup pots, thus preparing a dish fit for gourmets.

Worst of all, after eating the soup I still felt hungry, or even hungrier than before the distribution. "Don't worry kid, from that soup you will not grow", an old man smiled at me. Maybe he just looked old to me? But I did not want to grow, just to live! I envied the adults who were stronger than me. I don't know what devil got the better of me, but I volunteered to carry the empty barrel to be washed out. Maybe a scrap of food would fall my way. I hoped no one would grab the barrel-carrying pole away from me. Luckily the pole remained in my hand. The procession began to march in the direction of the washing house. I did not take into consideration my height, which was shorter than the other three pole-carriers. This caused the barrel to tilt down towards me and I had to hold up the pole with both arms.

I reached the destination, exhausted. I got into the barrel with the others to scrape out the scraps from the cracks, but to no avail. Someone had already done that before us on the field where the soup was distributed. After washing the barrel I stayed in the enormous wash house, where faucets and channels ran the length of the walls. I drank lots of cold water, which was a refreshing change from the faucets at the latrines in camp B.

The place was full of unfamiliar people from various barracks. There was also an entrance into the "washhouse" from another camp. The "washhouse" was located between camps A and B. It had two halls separated by a dividing screen. I stayed there a long time looking into the other camp. I don't know what I expected. I knew I needed to get back to my barrack. I didn't dare disobey the strict discipline, even though there was no list of names for the barrack. There was a daily count, but not one of us had a name or a number. No one realized that the barrack where I was living had "leftovers" from previous selections. I did not dare tell anyone that I was one of those "leftovers".

I got closer to the window. It seemed to me that people in the other camp were different from us. I was happy when I suddenly saw someone I recognized from Camp Sárvár in Hungary. He didn't remember me, but promised to look for my father. Shortly thereafter, my father appeared! Such excitement and joy... My father caressed me through the divider, tears streaming from his eyes. It was hard for him to believe that I was still alive. He was sure than I had already been taken "there". Elimination of the unfit was no secret. He told me that they were about to be taken to a work camp in the Auschwitz area. No one knew the details. While he talked he took a good-sized piece of bread from his pocket. I wondered how he had managed to get such a large piece and to keep it. He told me that prisoners sent to work get a full portion: one loaf divided between four or five people. It looked huge to me!

I did not take the bread from my father willingly, but hunger was stronger than any emotion. He warned me not to try saving it; people stole bread at every opportunity. He counseled me to be aware of what was going on in the camp. He had heard that people without numbers were also taken to work camps, and told me to try getting into one of those groups by any means possible. We had to part ways and return to our different camps. We agreed to meet the next day after soup distribution.

When I got back I met up with the two youths sharing the bunk with me. I felt uncomfortable telling them that I had met my father as neither one had relatives in the camp. I apologetically said that I probably would not see him again, because I did not want them to be jealous. I told my two friends that we had to make an effort to join the work groups, because we could not stay in the barrack indefinitely. There was something strange about these youths. They argued that they were worse off than me, that they were hungrier, and had been suffering from starvation longer than me, since the time they were in ghettos in Poland.

The next day, after soup distribution, I was so preoccupied with the bowl in my hands that I missed the opportunity to carry the barrels to be washed. I did not dare go there by myself to meet my father. It was far, and I was afraid to meet up with a *kapo*. The night was awful. I could not sleep because of the groaning. Some of the inmates were getting weaker. Many could not control themselves and did their "business" in the bunks. At least twice the overseers came with clubs to "calm things down". In the morning I could easily tell who had been beaten during the night. Blood was splattered on their skulls, and few took the trouble to wash up.

In the course of the day we were brought to the wash room in groups. There were no showers. The water dripped out of the faucets slowly and we could only wash our face and hands. While we were outdoors during the day the stench of our bodies was less noticeable. But at night, inside the crowded barrack, it was hard to get used to the filth and the stinking air. In the early hours after getting up, when it was still cold and dark, we would cluster together back to back, trying to get warm. Keeping warm was more important than avoiding the stench. Small talk was exchanged. We had no illusions about the chimneys surrounding the camp. The *Blockälteste* shouted at us all the time, in perfect German, "If you don't stand quietly during soup distribution you'll get to the chimneys fast!" One of the Block workers told us that most of the people in the Block were unfit for work. However it was the camp administration's decision when to hold an additional selection according to the amount of work at the crematoriums, which had to operate at top speed day and night.

The next day at noon I managed to volunteer to take the soup barrels back, and I was able to see my father again. I had finished eating the bread he had given me while keeping it out of sight. My father then asked me to wait. He returned several minutes later with some friends. We waited until the wash house was empty and then they pulled away the divider that separated us, and I passed over to their side. They warned me not to tell anyone about my "walk" because lots of people were ready to inform on others, even though they received nothing in return.

Here in Camp A everything was different. People wore more suitable clothes, including undershirts with sleeves. Everyone was clean. Many sat on benches located between the barracks, conversing between them. One person was playing German folk songs on an accordion. Unbelievable, it was a different world! I ran into the joker from Camp Sárvár who did card tricks. My father told me that within a few days they would be leaving for work camps. Until then, while they were waiting, the SS men came in the evenings for entertainment, listening to the music and enjoying the card tricks.

I cannot deny that I envied their sense of security because they were all assigned work. While I was talking to my father two of his friends tried to get the *Blockälteste* to give me a number on my arm so I could stay with them in Camp A. Of course the answer was negative. I heard them say that I was small, short, and too thin. "There is no point in taking a risk; there is no chance that he will be allowed to stay".

Before I returned to my camp, camp B, I received a slice of bread from one of my father's friends. It was a consolation because for me it was a lot. I promised my father that I would make every effort to get into a work group. We spoke frankly; if I didn't get into a group, I would not remain alive.

We said goodbye beside the wash house. That was my last meeting with my father. I never saw him again.

The Second Journey

All the rumors and dire prophesies proved to be true. Two days later the Germans took a transport from our barrack. The scene repeated itself: shouts, wailing, cruel beating from the SS and their underlings. Only two of us remained under the bunk. Waiting for morning was unbearable. At first we did not talk to each other. I did not even ask the youth where his friend had disappeared. Later he told me about the village where they had grown up together, and I noticed that he had also become indifferent to what was happening.

Nevertheless, he agreed with me that we had to get ourselves assigned to some work place. But how? What could we do? During my wandering around the camp I had learned that there were lots of "functionaries", but they were all older than me. All day long I asked myself how I could become one of them. I was in better shape than many others. I still had strength. I had not yet become weakened and worn out. The problem was that I was too young.

Towards evening I neared the barrack where the functionaries slept. I thought that someone would see me and offer me a job. Suddenly one of them came out, looked at me, asked what I was doing there, and began shouting "You look familiar!"

I ran away as fast as I could. I rushed into the mass of people between the barracks and decided not to take any more risks. What a stupid thing I had done! From now on I would keep my head down whenever I was near a *kapo* and the servants so they could not identify me. Even though I knew it was not a good idea to get far from my barrack, I had an urge to walk around some other barracks, to try my luck, to figure something out. Maybe I would find a work group to join. On one of these walks I saw in the distance people assembling on the roll call field.

I got closer and saw that they were arranging people into groups. The SS men and many functionaries were hurrying people to line up in rows. I saw that they were putting all the older and weaker people into one group. Those in the other group were younger and healthier-looking. In an instant I decided to join the long line. With a little luck I would succeed in getting into the latter group. Besides, what did I have to lose? They could always return me to my barrack... The selection went very quickly. Very few were assigned to the "good" group.

When I reached the head of the line I blessed the decision I had made: I was put into the group of the fit prisoners!

We were marched out of the camp very quickly, a group of just sixty. Only sixty people had survived that selection! We were taken to the railroad track. I had not seen the place since my arrival at Auschwitz. It was getting dark. We were put onto freight cars. Each of us received a large hunk of bread with a big piece of margarine. I had never seen such a delicacy in Auschwitz. We were immediately told that this would be our food for the next three days. I was glad that I had managed to get into a work group but sad that my father would not know. The journey began.

I tried to compare this trip to the first one from Hungary to Auschwitz. This one was much more organized. The freight car was divided in two, and we sat in rows the width of the car, each one sitting between the outspread legs of the prisoner behind him. We could not lean back; whenever someone tried, the whole line fell back and we fell on one another. The SS men sat in the space between the two halves in great comfort and boredom. Once in a while they would anger us with foul language, and make indecent remarks about the way we were sitting between each other's legs. In two corners of the car were containers for sanitary needs; those who sat nearby were very unfortunate.

No one knew where we were going and how long it would take to get there. The SS men ate their food greedily and loudly, while on the first day we already finished the bread that was supposed to last for three days. No point in taking chances. We were left with just water, and were satisfied with that. We could not sleep in the sitting position. Every time I leaned back the person in back of me pushed me forward so I would sit up straight.

In the evening the train stopped on a siding. The lucky ones sitting near the doors were commanded to empty the sanitary containers and to get water. We used the time to get up and stretch our legs. This created a lot of heated arguments, with people pushing, shoving, and complaining about their neighbors and the unbearable stench. The arguments turned into fights, but stopped immediately when the SS men entered the picture. It was a wonderful opportunity for them to repeat their usual game:

"Who got hit?"

And there was always a naïve prisoner who thought that justice would be done. He was taken out of line and commanded to point to the person who had hit him. The denials and pleadings of the accused were of no use. The 'hitter' and the "hittee" were taken to the space between the doors and the SS men forced them to hit each other until blood flowed. Only when they were both knocked out on the floor, somewhere between life and death, did the SS men have enough of the show, at which point they added a kick for the last round, and turned to other matters.

We were so exhausted that we fell asleep on top of each other. Except for the click-clack of the train cars and the whistle of the steam engine there was absolute silence the entire night. By the next morning we had become accustomed to the crowded seating arrangement. We were very hungry and regretted eating all the bread so hastily the first day, but mulling over regrets would not make us feel full…stomachs growling, stench rising, and the SS men did not stop cursing the damn stinking Jews. They had knapsacks full of food which they ate with great appetite, not letting our gaping stares bother them in the least. Once in a while they would throw a scrap of food out through the barred window. We became accustomed to their curses and indecent name calling. I began to think that maybe I really was a *"dreck zak"*, shitbag. I forced myself not to look at them, to avoid eye contact and not to arouse their attention.

We learned from prisoners familiar with the area that the train was going through the Sudeten Mountains, on the way to Germany. There was soup distribution at the next stop that day. What good news!

A large group of SS soldiers surrounded us during distribution. I think that only a madman would have tried to run away. There were not enough soup bowls for everyone. Each person who finished eating returned to the car. I used the opportunity to stretch out, breathe fresh air and look at the sky. I saw houses in the distance. Ordinary people probably lived there, eating and breathing normally. Did they care at all who was being transported in cattle cars, where they are being taken, and what would happen to them? After all we were only miserable Jews, *untermenschen*, (sub-human), and they probably had sons who were soldiers, fighting on the front for the purity of the race and for the *Reich*...

The fresh air I inhaled cost me dearly. When I got back onto the train car all the places were already taken except for a spot by the sanitary bucket. When people began climbing over me to reach the bucket I could not say anything. I knew that next time I would forego lingering outdoors. Were a few minutes of pleasure in the outdoors worth having your sleep interrupted the entire night?

When the train stopped for water on the third day, the SS men again allowed us to get out of the cars. We saw a beautiful ancient city in the distance, with towers capped with colorful domes, small one-story buildings and many churches. Someone identified the place as Dresden, one of Germany's ancient cities. He told us that we were nearing the province of Thuringia. In the afternoon we arrived at the new camp, and we learned that it was called Buchenwald.

3.

Buchenwald

We got off the cars and were marched through the entrance of the camp. Over the huge gate was a sign with a Nazi slogan.[15] I did not know how many train cars were packed with humans, but I could see an endless procession of prisoners entering the camp. We passed through the gigantic parade grounds near the gate and marched in an orderly fashion to the shower facility. The *kapos* calmed us, telling us that these were regular showers; that there were no gas chambers here. Here everyone goes to work. I was indifferent to that talk. Only one thing interested me: I had not eaten any bread for two days, and since yesterday's soup no food had entered our mouths.

The entire transport was herded into the showers of the disinfectant camp (quarantine). Waiting in line for the showers took a long time. I tried looking for someone I knew among all the people but did not recognize anyone. Looking around I saw that Buchenwald Camp was divided by fences into small camps, and that the long barracks were like those in Auschwitz, except that no furnace separated the barrack into two parts. Wherever you looked there was nothing, only bare dry ground, and a huge amount of barbed wire. No trace of a plant, a tree, a flower; the same barren dreariness as in Auschwitz. Talking

---

[15] The sign over the main entrance gate to Buchenwald gate read «Jedem Das Seine» which means «To Each His Own» or «Everyone Gets What He Deserves".

with people I learned that there were about 100,000 prisoners in Buchenwald, and that the camp had been operating since the Nazis came to power, and that it was used as a center from which workers were sent to various industrial areas in Germany. Food was the only thing I heard nothing about, except for the fact that it was distributed only after roll call. Looking at the line I asked myself how long it would take for everyone to get through. Maybe I would have the privilege of getting new clothes. I was missing buttons, and perhaps a little thinner since my pants kept slipping down. I would have to find a cord to tie them up, or I would lose my pants.

I was among the last to go into the shower, but I knew I wouldn't miss a thing; food would not be distributed without me. The line dragged on. I examined the faces of the prisoners around me. It seemed very strange that no one talked to anyone else. They were all immersed in themselves; there was nothing to talk about. Everything we needed to know had been said; everyone knew the routine for the day: shower, roll call, a portion of bread or soup... but something was nonetheless different - everyone here had tin bowls with two handles tied to the back of their pants. As they walked, the light red bowls swayed in step with their pace. If there are bowls, there is food! This equipment was clearly provided to the prisoners. Now that was a change to ponder. I turned to the left and said to the man standing beside me, a gray-haired adult, "Look, on the other side of the fence people are walking around with bowls!" He did not bother to answer. He continued mumbling to himself in Yiddish mixed with Polish. I understood that he was talking about a friend left behind somewhere. I shook him and demanded a response, but he did not react. It was as if he was detached from the surroundings and was in another place altogether. Many of the others were also staring off into space.

Perhaps I should start talking to myself? Perhaps that would help keep my mind off food? I had not thought about my family for a long time. I closed my eyes and could see them all in my imagination: father shaving with the strong-smelling RAZOL cream for Shabbat, which Mother loved… What other preparations were going on for Shabbat? I could not remember. My stomach ached, shriveled with hunger. I thought about my sister who got angry when my mother would spoil me. My sister was not at all fussy about food. She ate everything, even eating with gusto the skin that formed on the boiled milk. As for me, I was very picky and maybe that was the reason I was also very thin. At least one dish at every meal had to be something I liked, or I would refuse to eat. Who knows, perhaps someday in the future I would again be indulged with my favorite dishes?

The man beside me continued to chatter, full of complaints against his friend. I understood part of what he was saying: "I wanted to escape from the ghetto and my friend let me down and would not agree to risk it!" His monologue was over, and he glanced at me.

It was my turn to enter the shower. Like everyone, I threw my clothes onto a pile, except for the shoes which everyone hung on to in the shower. I was given some rough soap without scent or lather. Someone made a remark about the soap and the functionary answered, "There wasn't enough Jewish fat. That's why the soap has no lather!"

Lice

At least the water was hot. I could not recall the last time I had showered. When we had arrived at Auschwitz? So much time had gone by since then…after the shower we stood dripping, no towels, in line to get clothes. We got the same striped clothes. Everything was folded as if pressed in a mangle, reeking of disinfectant. I was glad to have clean clothes. Suddenly someone shouted: "Lice!"

And indeed, the pant seams were crawling with lice. I remembered that during the last days in Auschwitz I was scratching nonstop. Now I actually saw real lice with my own eyes. This did not bother me at all; if they gave us food, everything would be all right as far as I was concerned. After putting on the clothes everyone looked different to me. Suddenly I could not identify anyone who had been with me on the way here. That was because barbers working in a large hall had shaved everyone. There were only a few youths like me who had nothing to shave. I just had some thin fuzz along my face, where there had been *peyes* in bygone days.

A big surprise awaited us when we reached the registration table. They took passport pictures of us and filled out our personal details: name, place of birth, date of birth. I received a number on two strips of white cloth, along with another yellow strip (as did all the Jews) and a red triangle which had a "U" in the center, which meant that my country of origin was Hungary. We stood in line to have the numbers sewn onto our clothes. We were warned in no uncertain terms: "Each one will memorize his number in German. From now on, no one will be called by name, only by number!"

My number was 65295. I was happy; at last I had a number! Not on my arm, like my father, but at least a number! They must need us if they gave us numbers. I wanted to shout for joy: "Please, good father, tell everyone that Moshe-Yankel is alive and that he has a number on his clothes!"

See, I remembered you, my dear family. Were all my aunts and uncles also sent to Auschwitz? I wondered if they managed to hold out. Maybe they remained at home. Maybe only my family was sent to the concentration camp? My father was the only one in our entire family who was born in Slovakia. All the others were born in Hungary. Other memories of my family came back to me. For example, there was one uncle who liked to tease my mother because she was religious. "You are very righteous, Rozi", he would say, "so how is it that God doesn't help you a little more? You pray all day long, observe all the commandments carefully, try to raise a son to study Torah, and what do you get in return?" He would go on to add that he, who did not obey the commandments, enjoyed the good life, and that his wife had furs and diamonds while my mother had only the *Tzena Ure'ena* - sometimes called the Women's Bible this was a kind of household companion of portions of the Bible especially adapted for women.

As I daydreamt, registration was completed. We lined up again for roll call and this time the count went fast. We all anticipated the daily ration we received after roll call.

From the direction of the gate we heard the sound of drums, cymbals and wind instruments. I was stunned. A concert? Here, in this place? The *kapo* informed us that, "this is a well-organized concentration camp. There is an orchestra to make your lives pleasant as you leave for work and when you return. You had better learn the words!" He immediately began reciting the words to the marching song: *"Buchenwald, ich kann dich nicht vergessen, weil du mein Schicksal bist!"* - "Buchenwald, I cannot forget you, you are my destiny!"

The tune was imprinted in my memory from my stay in Buchenwald. Such excellent composers, such thoughtfulness of the Nazis… why not make life more pleasant for the *heftlinge* (prisoners)? Just like the lyrical and meaningful slogan at the entrance to the Auschwitz camp, "Work sets you free!"

Jokers had composed their own parodies of these songs. Back in Auschwitz I heard prisoners reciting the rhyme:

"Arbeit macht frei
    Crematorium eisns-twei-drei!"

In English: "Work sets you free, crematorium one-two-three!"

Roll call was completed, but the *kapos* announced that

food would be distributed only after we were organized in the barracks for the night. In the meantime we had to stand at attention, the camp commander was coming to give a speech. An entourage of SS men with dogs showed up. Occasionally during the speech they let the dogs run free, and they would pounce ferociously on the Jews in the back rows. We were in shock. Even though no one was bitten, the screams of terror were awful.

One of the SS men shouted, "*Achtung!*" (Attention), and immediately all was still.

"*Mitzen auf!*" (Hats off)

Everyone took off their hats, and the SS camp commander began speaking. "First of all, when you speak with an SS person remember that you must remove your hat, stand at attention, and keep your eyes to the ground. You are not worthy of looking a German in the face! Accursed Jews, if you want to continue living be as quiet as worms and lower than grass. Remember your numbers. If spoken to, identify yourselves by number. When approaching your superiors, recite your number and add 'I stand humbled'!" These were the words of greeting with which each transport was received.

Most of this was not new to me. In the previous weeks I had learned to keep a low profile, avoid the first row at roll call and not get caught glancing at the *kapos*. I saw what happened to those who did not adopt this behavior, and I learned that to stay alive I had to be invisible. Since my will to survive and hang onto life was very strong, I forced myself to follow the despicable rules imposed on us by those who governed our lives.

Finally we were brought to the barracks. I was in Block 56 where there were several young people my age. It was an enormous barrack, with three-tiered bunks similar to Auschwitz. The bunks had old straw mattresses crushed from use. All the new people were put in the top bunks. The lower bunks were already taken by the old-timers, which made no difference to me. I just needed to remember where my place was. Just one question bothered me: When would we receive food? The old-timers pointed to a separate room at the end of the barrack, the *kapos'* room. In there they divided up the bread, malevolently, into the smallest possible portions, and kept the remainder for bartering.

A roll call was held once again. The number of new inhabitants was recorded, and we became "citizens" of Block 56. Most of the people were from Poland. Luckily I was fluent in Yiddish and could easily communicate with them. They all wanted to know when I had been in Auschwitz and who had I met there, maybe by chance I had met someone they knew… I did not have answers to most of their questions; I had made very few acquaintances on my way to Buchenwald.

The Yiddish speakers warned me about the Ukrainian prisoners. Even though they were a minority in Block 56, they were the rulers, and the Block was known as the "Ukrainian Block". By this time I knew that the Ukrainians had absorbed their hatred of Jews with their mother's milk. They would attack us at every opportunity and they were no less cruel than the Nazis. You needed to be on the lookout for them and be careful around them. Since I always ate my bread immediately I had nothing to worry about; I had nothing except the clothes on my back.

The next morning at roll call we were told that the new people would work near the camp for a short period of time. I asked the old-timers when the soup would be distributed. They explained that everyone got soup where they worked. We received bread only at night, before going to sleep, just like at the other camps. The difference between this camp and Auschwitz was the orchestra that played to entertain the people on their way to work and back.

After several days there was an early wake-up call to go to work. I had no idea where we were going or what kind of work we were to perform. The group to which I was assigned had been there for a relatively long period of time. They showed me the palms of their hands, full of cuts and blue spots. This group almost always worked in the stone quarries in the area.

Leaving the camp for a remote work site was a change for me. It was a difficult trek. We marched on paths in a barren area toward large hills with glaring white peaks that stood out from a distance. When we got there we formed a human chain, and each person knew his assigned spot. We had to pick up stones and take them to a collection point where they were loaded and transferred to an unknown destination. I bent over and lifted stone after stone. I did not look around. SS men stood several meters away urging us to work faster. Some of them walked around with guard dogs.

By noon I was very discouraged. My hands were full of deep burning cuts. I wasn't even thinking about food... most of the prisoners were in constant fear that an SS man would give them a push as they carried a stone. I saw from a distance that sometimes a man carrying a stone would fall down, get kicked and screamed at by the guard, and struggle back on to his feet to return to work.

At noon break they gave us soup from huge containers. Everyone stood quietly and there was no shoving in line. I was not accustomed to such order. Did it come from exhaustion and fear of the dogs? An older man whom I had spoken with the day before stood beside me. He advised me to do whatever I could to avoid working in the quarry. He probably felt sorry for me and was trying to help me. "This work is not for a skinny little skeleton like you", he said. I did not need his advice to realize that I would never last at this kind of work

We continued to work until evening. The day seemed endless and I thought it would never end. We returned from work drained and exhausted. Most of us did not have the strength to wash up. Completely worn out and weary I remained outside the barrack, since we were not allowed inside until after bread distribution. I leaned against the wall, my weary brain empty of any thoughts.

Slowly recovering I got up and decided to go to the large latrine before bread distribution. The latrine was exactly like the one at Auschwitz, but with more activity. I was told that all camp "business" took place here. As I sat down on the channel wall I reminded myself that I was wearing new clothes from the Buchenwald storehouse, and that I had to take care of them since I would not be given any other items. It was a topic that deserved serious attention: how to keep my pants clean when there was no paper with which to wipe. It was no wonder that we all stank to high heaven.

I loitered in the latrine for quite a while, watching how business was done. It was all based on promises: one-half serving of soup tomorrow for a cigarette. I did not smoke yet and I couldn't understand how anyone would give up in advance a half-portion of soup for a cigarette. The Ukrainians in Block 56 sold cigarettes for portions of soup or bread. And not only cigarettes: a Ukrainian speaking to me in German tried to sell me a homemade bread knife. I asked him why I would want a knife and he explained that I could cut my bread into portions so I could enjoy it much longer. The Ukrainians made the knives by sharpening soup spoon handles on stone, and they were amazingly sharp. I did not buy anything. The Ukrainian asked me where I kept my daily bread, and I answered that I ate it immediately.

"*Verfluchter Jude* (damned Jew), you learned how to live!", he screamed at me. I quickly got away from there, feeling proud of myself. Look, I was smart, I had learned to live, maybe I would manage to survive.

Bread distribution and the sleep that followed made me feel better. The next day I got up feeling encouraged as I went out to work in the quarry. I was lucky that day – assigned to an area that was more level than the previous day, so that it was easier for me to hold the rocks and hand them to someone else. Also, the soup I got was thicker than the day before. The friendly adult again urged me not to take any chances, and try to find different work… as if it depended on me. I knew I had no way of getting out of working in the quarry. Maybe they would transfer us to a different place or maybe by chance I would be assigned to less strenuous work, but in the meantime I had to continue toiling.

In the Block I was very concerned about the dominance of the Ukrainian thugs. They gave us, the Jews, no peace, cursing and shoving us at every opportunity. Their job in the Block was to collect the corpses. At night they would go from barrack to barrack, collecting the bodies into big metal-lined wagons. The old-timers told me that the Ukrainians took the clothes off the dead, threw the naked bodies into the wagons, and took them to the crematorium to be burned. Now I understood how the Ukrainians had so much "merchandise" to sell in the latrines.

One morning, to my surprise, we did not go out to work. The explanation I received was that in Germany it was customary to have a "rest day" every two weeks. There was no reason to rejoice in the possible prospect of rest. Early that morning we were rushed into dragging the mattresses outside in order to shake them out and clean them. The old-timers warned me not to be too energetic since the mattress was only a bag of crumbling straw. It was hard to lay on it because it was so worn.

I waited in the yard for the barrack to be washed out so I could put my mattress back in place, and would not have to protect it so it would not be stolen. When I was not thinking about food I scratched myself. I quickly discovered that during the day, when I stood in the sun, the warmth roused the lice that began to celebrate. The seams and folds of my clothes were teeming with lice. As a newcomer I had no chance of getting a change of clothes. Only the old-timers, with permanent places of work, were so fortunate.

I joined a long line near the showers. Maybe something was being distributed there? When my turn came I found out that I was not yet eligible for a haircut. Not much hair had grown back since my head had been shaved in Auschwitz. I also did not need a shave. The barber sized me up and said, "*Boychik*, come back next year and I'll shave the fuzz off your face!"

Time crept by painfully slowly. I wanted to do anything that would take my mind off food. I did not know whether we received soup on the days we did not go to work. I had no friends or acquaintances and I felt lonely. You couldn't just go up to another prisoner and tell him that you felt lonely and would like to talk to him. How would I pass the time until evening? If I had a friend I could exchange stories with him, tell him about happy times at home, picture along with him that perhaps a miracle would take place and this would all come to an end, and try to guess together with him what was happening outside, in the big world…I thought that if I could get through this nightmare and manage to stay alive, at least I could say that I had been in Germany. In fact I had really not seen anything except a quarry, freight cars and gray barracks, but nevertheless I would have something to tell.

My pants were hanging loose on me. Every day I drew in the cord. It appeared that I was getting thinner every day. My hip bones ached every morning. If only there was a little more straw in the mattress I would not feel my bones as much. At least I could sleep. They say that you don't feel hunger when you are asleep… Here we go again thinking of food! Maybe today, in honor of the "day of rest", they would give us something extra? Maybe I would be lucky and get an overflowing ladleful of thick soup? I vowed that when I returned home safely I would even drink milk! I recalled that the day before, on the way to the quarry, I had seen a vegetable garden by the offices. Oh, what beautiful radishes could be grown in a garden.

Okay, I'll go for a stroll in the latrine, maybe I'll hear

something interesting. Last time I did that I heard that once in a while they needed volunteers for various jobs. Now I have more seniority so maybe I'll get something. I noticed errand boys running around between the Blocks, washing plates, polishing boots. These were the *stube-dienste* [16], the kapo's assistants, and they all looked plump. The only thing we had in common were the prisoner clothes we all wore. In return for their services they received more food than I did. I did not hear or find anything interesting in the latrine. I had gone for nothing.

Finally the roll call before soup distribution was held on the field beside the barrack. It turned out to be a good day after all. I don't know what was in the soup, but it was warm! The taste was indefinable and it was impossible to identify the ingredients. But my belly was full. This was the first time I had received soup at the camp, since up until now we had only been fed at the quarry. Here no one rushed me. Ah, it was a "day of rest" today, with plenty of time to eat the soup and lick the bowl on all sides. The afternoon went by with less difficulty, and I didn't even want to rest on the bunk. It was truly "a good day".

Laboratory Experiments

During evening roll call before bread distribution something unfamiliar happened. When roll call broke up we were commanded to line up single file before entering the barrack. An SS man accompanied by two helpers dressed in prisoner

---

[16] *Stube-dienst – a kapo's assistant.*

clothes stood beside the entrance. The German selected people, recording their personal number. My number was also recorded. After bread distribution I found out that the SS person had selected ten young people. My bunkmate reassured me that nothing bad would come of my number being recorded. If I had not done anything that called for punishment, I had nothing to worry about.

The next morning, during the lineup before leaving for work, I became aware of a miracle that had befallen me. The *kapo* announced that those whose number had been recorded were to remain in the barrack and would not be going to the quarry. The Block worker told us to stay in the barrack until we were called. At midmorning a runner came with the list of our numbers and commanded us to follow him. We did not ask where we were going.

Within a few minutes we were in a new area of the camp: the same barracks but with a few small gardens around them. The longest barrack was used as the camp hospital. I had heard rumors that very few actually got better there. None of us could guess why we were called here. When we were selected we had assumed that young men were needed for work.

The place was very quiet. There were no shouting *kapos* here. We were shown into a large room and seated on benches, somewhat surprised by the humane treatment we were suddenly receiving. Soon a man appeared who I assumed was a doctor by the stethoscope in his pocket. He explained that the clinic needed us for one week. We were to come to the inside gate every morning. If we behaved well we would receive a bowl of soup from their kitchen. For a bowl of soup I was willing to do anything!

One by one we were brought into the doctor's room. I do not know what tests were given to the others. The doctor checked my blood pressure, and then told me to get undressed. He looked at the skin on my face and between my legs with a magnifying glass. He made a face during the exam. My hygiene apparently did not please him.

"*Verfluchter schwein*" (damned swine) were the only words that came out of his mouth.

The aide laid me down on the sofa and the SS doctor gave me several injections. They did not hurt, or perhaps I ignored it all. I had no idea what the injections were for, and even if I knew that I was being used for experiments I could not object. The list with our numbers and Block number was on the doctor's desk. After administering the shots he wrote something on the list and I was sent out.

We gathered together and walked towards the kitchen. No one spoke, or asked what had happened to the others. As promised, we got a bowl of soup. Not since leaving my home did I remember such a heavenly taste. It was real soup, with flavor and aroma, and the ingredients could be identified. Unbelievable!

We returned to Block 56, revived. Even the *Blockälteste* treated us like humans, allowing us to rest on the bunks whenever we felt like it. Now the days passed quickly. I was regaining my strength and I did not know how or whom to thank for my good luck.

One of the adults who returned from the quarry asked me about what had transpired at the camp hospital. It seemed that everyone knew that we were being treated at the hospital. He was very friendly, and told me I did not have to volunteer to go there. As if I had a choice after they recorded my number! So far I felt fine, and I was very hopeful. The soup was worth everything and I began to think that I wouldn't have to go back to the quarry, because the very thought of going back there depressed me terribly. And if I went back, at least I will have gained weight this week, and become stronger from the excellent soup.

The man told me that the discipline at work was becoming more oppressive. He himself was covered with black and blue marks. SS men hit the workers indiscriminately, and every day more and more prisoners died from the beatings.

He was the only person in Block 56 I could talk to, even though we never asked each other personal questions. There was a silent agreement between us not to talk about home, bygone days, or even that the war may end some day and we would be free again. "Freedom" was too illusory to talk about. Once, when I told him that at home life certainly continued as before, he replied: "Listen boy, don't deceive yourself. In the new world the Germans are the strong ones and rule the universe, and all the other Peoples work for the Third Reich. There is no chance that we will make it out of here alive".

I did not want to listen to that gloomy prediction. I wanted to think that in spite of everything we would get out of here. Over and over I imagined how I would tell everyone that I had held up, and here I was, still alive! Back in Auschwitz I had realized that the weak and the old had no hope of surviving. I had managed to get through two selections and I came very close to becoming nothing but ashes…

That week we were free after the daily treatment at the hospital, and during the day I frequently saw the Ukrainians transporting the corpses. Once, while I was standing in the latrine, one of them said to me, "Don't worry lousy Jew, you'll soon be in my wagon too!" Even though I was used to their violent hatred I answered, "Aren't you a prisoner too?" In reply he gave me a firm smack, and from then on I avoided any encounter with the Ukrainians.

On the seventh and last day the aide ordered us to stay in the Block after the treatment. Although we missed the soup we gained one more day of not working in the quarry. Meanwhile, the physical condition of the quarry workers worsened considerably. Many were wounded, some were limping, but they went to work despite it all, instead of going to the sick rooms for treatment. Rumor had it that it didn't pay to go to those rooms because no one came out alive. Every few days new people came to the barrack to replace those missing, so that the work group always went out in full force. I marveled at the punctuality of the new transports. How German pedantry managed to count the fallen and immediately replace the missing numbers!

I became friendly with one of the boys with me at the clinic. He was from Poland so we didn't have many common topics of conversation. Even so, the value of conversation was unimaginable, empty of content though it was, in the terrible loneliness of the camp. The boy was impressed that I was so interested in what was happening, and that I knew everything going on in Block 56. He himself was indifferent and took no interest in what was going on around him, or the question of what fate awaited us. Most of the time he sat against the wall of the Block and just dozed. When I asked him what he was thinking about he replied: "About nothing. Sometimes I dream about the portion of bread we will get this evening".

I tried to get him to talk. I wanted him to tell me about his past life. I ached to hear how people had once lived normal lives when there was no war. But he asked me not to bother him, because all he wanted was to doze, and just listening to me was too great an effort for him. I left him alone.

I was afraid of the silence. Yet all the same some things I did ignore. I never asked who had been taken away in a wagon, who had died, or the cause of anyone's death. I knew the answer anyway. Apparently they all died for no reason, they just "fell asleep" from exhaustion. There were times when I too was desperately afraid of "falling asleep".

At evening roll call the *kapo* had a list of those of us who had been selected to go to the camp hospital. We were ordered to report there in the morning. Well, this was a welcome change, tomorrow I will be occupied going back and forth from the hospital. I will certainly get soup too, and I will be really full!

The next morning we showed up at the entrance to the

hospital. Everything followed the same routine, except we did not get any injections. The doctor examined me from head to toe with a magnifying glass, made a few notes and handed the list with our numbers to the aide.

We were sent back to Block 56 and told that we might be called back in a few days. We did not get any soup, but we took comfort in the fact that at least we wouldn't have to go out to work. I thought that everything was going well. Who knew what shape I would have been in if I had worked at the quarry the past few days!

An Opportunity

A few days went by, and luckily I was not sent back to work in the quarry yet. Every evening I would wait for the group to return from work. When the orchestra began to play "The Buchenwald Song" I would get close to the parade grounds and study those who returned. Their condition worsened daily. Most of them could barely drag themselves onto the camp grounds. Would I also have a similar fate, or perhaps I would get lucky and be sent to a work group at a less terrible place?

The next day a large group of new prisoners arrived. They were not housed in our barrack, and were told to stand at the end of the field. I sensed that something new was developing. I overheard two *kapos* saying that the new people would not be housed in the camp. They were to be sent to a work group in Germany. A ray of hope filled my heart. Here was an opportunity to get out of Buchenwald! Meanwhile, the group was taken to be disinfected, washed, and recorded; the same routine I had also gone through.

After next day's roll call I was still free to wander. I got closer to the new ones grouped in the field and nonchalantly joined them. I found out that they had not yet been assigned a work group and that most of them did not know one another. I could loiter in their midst without drawing attention. The fact that they were kept apart in a separate field gave me hope that this transport would indeed go to the industrial area of Germany.

Suddenly the SS men appeared and began hurrying the large group toward the gate. I was in one of the rows so that even if I had wanted to go back I couldn't. If all went as expected, I thought to myself, within a few hours I would be on a freight train headed towards Germany. We were indeed headed towards the railroad tracks, and I was in a good mood. I knew that any work place would not be as terrible as the quarry. I was also growing concerned about the "treatments" at the hospital clinic, and felt that I needed to get away from there, the sooner the better.

I walked energetically along with the group. I wanted to share my joy with somebody but I did not see any boy my age. We reached the freight train, and maintaining strict order the Germans divided us into groups. We stood silently. I was so preoccupied thinking about my happiness that I did not notice that the person standing beside me had asked me twice why there was a smile on my face and why I looked so satisfied. I did not answer. I dared not tell him about my experiences in Block 56. No one was to know that I had left without permission!

A big wagon similar to those that took corpses from Block 56 stood at the edge of the field, loaded with loaves of bread. Before getting on the freight train every prisoner received a relatively large portion of bread with a lump of marmalade. We all marveled at the marmalade. When was the last time I had seen jam?

I knew from experience that it was best to position myself near the door. That way when it opened from time to time I would be able to see outside and even breathe some fresh air. As soon as I settled down near the door I ate the marmalade, after all it could fall off the bread. I was used to the shoving and crowding. I sat close to the car opening and resisted any attempt to move me away. Here and there angry shouts and complaints were heard. Lumps of marmalade fell to the floor of the car and people fought to salvage the precious delicacy.

Two SS men entered the car and made room for themselves with the help of clubs and rifles. Total stillness reigned at the sight of them. Their appearance was enough to stifle all arguments and complaints. The train engine began moving and I began to breathe easier - I had escaped from the quarry at Buchenwald!

The trip passed rather quietly. Occasionally the bored SS men would roar, "Damn Jews, stop stinking!" Yet they kept their distance to avoid the stench we gave off. They got close only to hit us and then, surprisingly, the smell did not faze them. Was it any wonder that we stank? Could we be expected to smell like perfume when we could not bathe, change clothes, or wipe ourselves after going to the toilet? We prisoners got used to the stench. The entire time I was in the camps I never heard a complaint about the filth and the foul odors. The lice that plagued us were a thousand times worse. They caused us untold misery. While I sat quietly they would run all over my body with delight, biting everywhere. What torture! We all scratched ourselves endlessly. I looked forward to the minute the train would come to a stop so I could get off, stretch, and it would be easier to scratch myself.

The person sitting next to me could not restrain himself. He suddenly stood up and announced that he had to urinate immediately. The Nazi laughed maliciously and ordered him to hold it. "We'll reach the camp in three hours. It's not so bad; you will survive!" The man insisted, and the SS person cracked the car door open and shouted, "Lousy Jew, go pee!"

The man stood at the narrow opening, dropped his pants,

and tried to do his business while the train was moving. The strong wind sprayed the urine back on him. He returned and sat down in wet clothes. The SS man was happy. He turned to his partner and said loudly: "Did you see how that Jew wet himself?" He then asked if anyone else wanted to pee. The others saw what had happened and did not want to undergo the same experience. It was easier to just wet your pants - why stand in the wind to get the same result?

One of the prisoners started the rumor that we were going to Berlin. I did not take it seriously. My thoughts were elsewhere: Was this the final station? Would I last out the war at the new place? Would the work conditions be less torturous than at the quarry? And most important, how would I avoid their beatings? I could perhaps get the better of hunger; I had never been big and fat. If only I could avoid being finished off by the kicking or the beatings. If only I managed to stay alive - I will have so much to tell! Yet will they believe me when I tell them that in the camps all Jews were equal, poor and rich, foolish and wise. A person's family lineage or the size of his house meant nothing. Here, in this new world, only one thing mattered: the ability to survive. And to do that you had to guard your allotment of bread and avoid getting beaten.

Perhaps I was mistaken and we were the only ones still alive? Perhaps no one will be left to hear all the horror stories? Could the Germans be so strong that they ultimately win and only they and their allies survive? I was completely confused. I would be better off scratching myself instead of philosophizing. The lice were very energetic. At home I was told that only Gypsies had lice. That myth was proved wrong: Jews also suffer from lice.... I dozed off despite everything.

4.

Magdeburg - A Camp in Germany

The train came to a screeching halt, making us all jump. The SS man announced that we would all get off soon. His tight-lipped partner, trying to display a sense of humor, announced: "*koffers die nehmen mit!*" (take your suitcases with you!), a standard announcement at German train stations. We hurried to get off and arranged ourselves as usual in groups of five. Tarpaulin-covered trucks were waiting for us, and we got on after we were counted. The ride did not take long. The signs we saw along the way indicated that we were in Magdeburg. We reached an area where the houses were farther apart, and saw a sign pointing to Rotenza. We were there within five minutes, and could see the barracks from a distance. We knew: this was a new concentration camp.

One difference was immediately noticeable: when we got off the trucks we saw that we were in the midst of an urban area. I actually saw citizens walking in the street, next to the fenced camp. I was very happy to be in an inhabited environment, not like Auschwitz or Buchenwald, where all you could see were barracks and barbed wire up to the horizon. Here regular people were out and about. We reached an industrial area, just as we were promised in Sárvár. For a moment I forgot the rumbling in my stomach. I had a chance to live!

As we neared the entrance to the camp I looked around. There were military barracks on one side of the camp and houses several stories high on the other side. The residents, including women and children, could easily be seen standing by their windows: a real civilian population!

We entered the camp in groups and joined about one hundred people who were already standing in the line-up. We were on the parade grounds facing the civilian homes. It was still light outside so we could clearly see them watching us curiously. There was higher ground at the front of the parade grounds, forming an elevated area. SS officers stood there talking to each other. Dozens of *kapos* and functionaries ran around the grounds, clubbing the prisoners to urge them to line up quickly for roll call.

I immediately realized that in this sense the place was no different from the other camps. The beatings did the job, as lines formed quickly in absolute silence. Dog barks were suddenly heard coming from the direction of the entrance gate. An SS officer appeared on the elevated area and received the following report, delivered in a thunderous voice: "The Jews are lined up by barracks and the total number is two thousand eight hundred prisoners!"

The SS officer gave us a furious look and delivered his speech:

"This is a work camp. We have no gas chambers. You are here among the citizens of the Reich. Behave accordingly, work loyally – and live!" He ended his speech with a sentence that I had heard at Buchenwald: "Be as quiet as reptiles, and as low as grass, and you will live".

I wondered about the source of this exhortation, proclaimed at every camp. Were these the words of a contemporary German philosopher?

After roll call we were taken to the showers, where two surprises awaited us. First, we were given soap, and as if that were not enough, the soap was sudsy! There were three small

Latin letters cut into the bar: r, j, f – which I was told was an acronym for the German words "*rein judische fett*", meaning "pure Jewish fat". The second surprise was the special haircuts we got. Every prisoner had a stripe shaved around his skull from the back of his neck to his forehead. I asked why they didn't give us a full haircut since we were full of lice. I was told that this was a way to prevent us from escaping the camp. This struck me as ridiculous; where could we escape to from here? It was done to humiliate us. I don't know how the others felt but it did not bother me. We did not get clean clothes, but were instructed to take care of the clothes of the Third Reich we had been given before.

After the shower I felt a piercing hunger. I took comfort in the fact that we would soon go into the barracks and receive our bread ration. There were many functionaries at the camp to make sure that strict order was maintained near each barrack, so that distributing the bread and entering the barrack proceeded quickly, which pleased me. I got the upper bunk, and since there were not too many people I could roll over instead of lying all night without moving. On the other hand, the distance between the bunk and the ceiling was very small, making it impossible to sit up. I finished eating my bread lying down. I decided to continue my habit of eating the bread we received all at once, not dividing into smaller pieces to last for several meals. I knew from experience that my stomach was the safest place for bread.

I began to examine my bunkmates. Up until now no bond had been formed between us. No one knew what to expect the next day, what work we would get, and where. When the lights were turned off we were forbidden to leave the barrack. There were no guards in the camp, but we obeyed the order. I fell asleep and did not wake up during the night. This was a big change from the previous camps.

We were awakened early. Roll call was conducted under floodlights and took two hours. The lineup was conducted by the *lagerälteste* [17], the senior camp prisoner. I did not see SS men inside the camp. Those who had arrived here a month before told us that the SS men and the camp commander showed up only in the evenings when the prisoners came back from work. The *kapos* told us that each work group had a head *kapo* and several assistants. They began to divide us into work groups. One *kapo* announced that he needed eighty men. Another announced that he needed two hundred workers, and so on. When a work group had the requisite number of workers the extra men joined another group. On the first day no one knew where his group was going. I joined the group of two hundred prisoners; my survival instinct told me it was better to be in a large group.

Before leaving we were given coffee. This was something new! The coffee was actually muddy and tasteless, but at least we had something warm in our stomachs. Like at Buchenwald, each person carried his bowl tied to the back of his pants.

We started out. The SS men joined the groups at the camp gate. It was a summer day, and for us walking along the road in broad daylight was a new experience. The *kapos* tried to teach us German songs. The SS men accompanying us sang along with the group, and once in a while urged us to join in. So idyllic!

We reached the factory together with many German workers who rode bicycles to work. Apparently we were the first prisoners to come to work there. The Germans gave us a quick glance without saying a word.

The factory was called Brabag (*Brankole Benzine Fabrik*). It was an oil refinery. We saw that it had been bombed recently and some parts had been destroyed. We were divided into small groups, and our job was to clear the rubble using wheelbarrows and to clean the bricks which would be reused. The work was grueling. There were few younger workers, and the older ones had a hard time keeping up with the workflow dictated by the

---

[17] *Lagerälteste* - camp leader or camp senior.

German overseers. The SS men hurried us by hitting us with their rifle butts or kicking us.

The break for food came as a real deliverance. It lasted half an hour and we received the usual thin soup. The people in my group were sprawled on the ground exhausted. Three SS men sat nearby and harassed us.

"Accursed Jews, you have it good here! Lying on the ground resting! You get three meals a day. Why don't you work better?"

Of course no one dared answer. We were forbidden to talk to the SS, and besides we really did get three meals: black coffee in the morning, thin soup at noon and a piece of bread at night…

On the way back from work I learned about something that would be a daily occurrence. Coming towards us was the night shift work group on its way to a factory. In a mixture of languages, mainly Yiddish, Polish and Hungarian, they reported the size of the bread portion that would be distributed that day: one loaf for five people (about 200 grams per person), or one loaf for six people (about 160 grams per person). We knew ahead of time what size to expect that night.

Returning to camp from the factory took a lot longer than getting there in the morning. We were all bone-tired from the exhausting work. The SS men wanted to get back to their quarters as quickly as possible, and they hustled the laggards impatiently by kicking them. The camp gate opened and we all breathed a sigh of relief. We had made it through the first day of work!

The lineup did not take long, and afterwards I could barely drag myself to the bath house to wash my face. I gave up on the idea of walking around the camp and getting a closer look at the electric fence around us. I went to bed and fell asleep immediately, once again not making the acquaintance of my fellow bunkmates.

The next morning was different. Everyone talked about

where they had worked the day before and people quickly decided where it would be better to work today. After morning roll call there was complete chaos. The *kapos* stood in different places on the grounds and called out the names of the factory assigned to each work group. Everyone began shoving, trying to reach the "best" groups. The noise of the squabbles was dreadful, and the *kapos* did not intervene. They did not care who got into which group. Lights went on in the houses outside the camp and the curious citizens watched the scene.

Suddenly a sharp whistle was heard. The camp elder appeared on the grounds and immediately everything was quiet. He threatened that a new system for breaking up into work groups would be implemented the next day. That was enough to frighten and worry us. People lined up quietly in groups and I did not regret returning to the Brabag group. I was not among those running around, because I did not have a clue where it would be better to work. I was happy to avoid the skirmishes that broke out on the question which group to join. At this point I made peace with the hard work. After all, compared to the hard labor at the quarry at Buchenwald, the work at Brabag was much easier.

As it was a long way to work we were already tired when we arrived. I estimated that we walked four kilometers in each direction every day. Not being able to have a conversation was very upsetting to me. The SS ignored prisoners who talked among themselves; their concern was that we walk fast. But it was impossible to enter into a conversation with a person walking beside me.

During the day I gave a lot of thought to what would happen to the older people in the group. How would they last if already on the second day they no longer had the strength to continue? The fact that we had to hold up those that could not walk on their own troubled me. Most of the prisoners were tired of dragging the weak ones back to camp, but they had no choice. If someone refused to hold them up the SS men would quickly kick and hit him, teaching him to "help his fellow-man". For them the most important thing was to return to camp with the exact same number of prisoners with which they had left in the morning. They kept this rule meticulously. I saw people in other groups also dragging those who could not walk on their own.

All the groups lined up for roll call. The men who could no longer stand were placed at the side of the grounds to be counted, because the numbers had to match. Many times the lineup was more tiring than the work we did: we were so close to bread distribution and so far from the end of the roll call...

Immediately after the count came the "punishment hour". Anyone who had broken a rule during the day was punished in front of everyone, so that we would know what happened when any rule is violated, even slightly. A prisoner who talked to a civilian worker instead of listening to the work supervisor, a prisoner who used the civilian bathroom instead of our specially-prepared latrine - any prisoner who committed any infraction no matter how insignificant - was considered by the Germans to be a criminal who needed to be punished publicly.

Therefore, during "punishment hour" the *kapos*, who wanted to show their loyalty to the Germans, were more brutal than their masters. They walked around writing down the numbers of those considered to have committed a so-called infringement. At the appointed time the camp commander and his dog would appear, and the *kapo* would call out numbers from his list. The lucky ones got their punishment from the camp elder. His slaps were stinging and he would finish with a push that brought the prisoner to the ground, but the prisoner could get back up and into the line without real damage done to him. But woe to those who fell into the hands of the other *kapos*. They would pound their clubs all over a person's body and would not ease up until their unconscious bloody victim was beaten to the ground and could no longer get up.

The "difficult" prisoners, by German standards, received

their punishment from the *Lagerführer* [18], the camp commander whom we called "the dog trainer". The show was short: the trainer would pull the dog's leash and whisper something in his ear, and the dog would attack the person and tear him to shreds with his teeth. The unconscious prisoner would remain on the ground for hours, until someone would take the trouble to bring him to the sick room. I do not know who among those attacked remained alive, as in the first days at the Magdeburg I did not know most of the prisoners. During the lengthy punishment hour the windows of the civilian houses outside the camp would open and the civilians would stand there to watch the "daily entertainment show".

There was much tension the next morning before we split into work groups. The camp commander had ordered the groups we considered to be good to stand near the electric fence. People did not dare to approach the fence for fear of being electrocuted, so no one rushed to get into these groups. Unwillingly, I returned to the Brabag group. Work was hard and time dragged by very slowly. The bored SS guards looked for any excuse to harass the weak ones in the group.

One morning, while groups were being sent to various locations in the factory, the *meisters* [19] arrived. These were German citizens responsible for specific jobs, and they chose me and several other youths to work in the workshop. They taught me to drill holes in steel rails. I was very pleased. Here no one could rush me. The SS man whose job it was to guard us stood at the entrance to the shelter and watched, but did not bother us. All day long I tried to figure out how I could manage to get here the next day as well, but I did not succeed. The minute we saw the *meister* coming we ran toward him. The SS man, who noticed our enthusiasm, placed others in the group instead of us, and the *meister* did not object.

---

[18] *Lagerführer* - the head SS officer assigned to a particular concentration camp who served as the commander of the camp.

[19] *Meister* - German citizen who was responsible for a specific job in the factory.

Time went by very slowly. At the camp nothing ever changed. It seemed to me that the SS men looked forward to the end of the day, to the "punishment hour" after the count. It was impossible not to notice that the number of barrack inhabitants dwindled from day to day. There were days when more than ten bodies or unconscious prisoners were carefully laid out for the count at the side of the grounds. Sometimes I would talk to my friend about our wretched situation. How long could we hold out?

The days grew shorter and the nights got colder. Even though each of us had a blanket, we tended to wrap ourselves up together on the bunks to keep warmer. The morning chill was harsh when we got up. We got used to standing back to back to keep each other warm. This angered the *kapos* and brought blows with clubs for those who "spoiled the lineup rows".

One morning I decided to change my luck and join a different group. This group worked in the gas plant. Later I sorely regretted my impetuousness. While working in the group that day I figured out that every day this group was made up of prisoners who did not fit into the other work places. We worked without almost any break, carrying steel bars or pushing wheelbarrows with coal. I never looked to see exactly what was produced in this factory. The entire plant was made of gigantic framed units that housed steam tanks. Our job was to bring the coal to one of these tanks. The problem was that the civilians overseeing us oppressed us no less than the SS guards. I overheard a German civilian talking to an SS man about the Jewish slave laborers, asking him why they brought such weak youngsters who had no strength to push a wheelbarrow. The SS man did not respond.

At noon we were given cold thin soup. Some prisoners were so weak they could not get up after the break. It took several kicks from the SS men for them to drag themselves back to work with their last ounce of strength.

While lining up to walk back I heard the German civilian

ask the SS man to bring stronger prisoners the next day. The SS man just shrugged his shoulders and said, "They are all the same".

The entire way back I thought about German stupidity. If they gave us more food, we would have more energy at work. But then I thought that in fact the issue of work did not interest the SS men. As far as they were concerned all the Jews could drop dead. That was the lofty goal of Nazi Germany. More than once I heard from the *kapos* in camp that no more Jews were left in the world. Those who were not yet dead were in forced labor camps building the great Reich. Maybe he was right? Could it be possible that no Jews were left in the free world? If so, perhaps it was truly not worthwhile to struggle to survive day after day.

Escape Attempt

One day, as we were lugging heavy poles on our shoulders at Brabag, one pole slipped off my shoulder and scraped my arm, causing it to bleed. In the evening, after the general counting, I went to the sick line. Actually it was not a sick line. Whoever needed attention stood in line by the clinic. The line was long but the service was quick. We recognized the orderly who came to the camp grounds each evening when the prisoners in need of attention were dragged to the sick room. By the time my turn came I was frightened. I saw many people whose wounds became infected within a few days (at camp this was called *phlegmona*). These wounds rarely healed because of the total lack of vitamins from which we suffered. There were dozens of people in the camp with wounds oozing pus. I hoped I would not reach that point. The clinic smelled of pus. Every so often a *kapo* would come in to hasten the treatment.

The treatment I received was very simple. The orderly did not disinfect the wound or put salve on it. He only bandaged my arm with tissue paper. While at the clinic I saw him amputate infected fingers. We were told that this was the only way to get cured. Aside from the paper bandages they also distributed charcoal powder for diarrhea. Obviously, not one single item there could be called "medication". According to camp lore, people with ties to the camp administration confiscated the alcohol intended for disinfectant. It was their main source of the ingredient used to make schnapps, which the Germans needed so badly. Every evening we heard drunken singing in German coming from the staff barracks.

In the latrines I would see how the functionaries did business, selling items from the general kitchen. Of course, even though we knew they were stealing from the rations intended for us, there was nothing we could do about this. Sometimes the thought crept into my mind that perhaps they were right: maybe we, the Jews, were only sub-human? These desperate thoughts were the result of the constant debasement we suffered from all and at every level. I was especially concerned that many prisoners among us showed signs of losing their mental capacities, extremely apathetic throughout the daily routine. By now I had become very well acquainted with my bunkmates, but with the passing of each day I was able to communicate with them less and less.

Autumn had come and the weather turned rainy. We returned from work soaked, and standing at roll call wreaked havoc on all of us. Many would collapse. We lost count of the number of dead. All we wanted was for the standing at the count to finally come to an end so that we could go to the barracks. The stench in the barracks was intolerable, but at least it was warm inside. Even after a light rainfall our clothes grew clammy, forming clouds of vapor, but we would dry out during the night.

At morning lineup the coughing was so noisy that it interfered with the count. We became accustomed to the *kapo* moving through the rows, listening for the coughers and giving them a few blows to quiet things down.

One day it so happened that I did not leave for work. That morning one of the camp staff grabbed me by the throat, dragged me out of the work group, and told me he needed me to help in camp. I did not realize that every day several people were kept back to clean the latrine or to do any other work the *kapo* in charge would think up.

I was sent to the clinic. I was received by a prisoner, neat, shaved, and well-dressed. I had seen him occasionally during the official rest days. I never got near him. He was from Hungary and I had heard that sometimes he would do a favor for Hungarian Jews and give them occasional work. I did not know what his exact status was in camp, but I noticed that the SS men sometimes spoke with him.

When we got to the clinic four of us were given a large stretcher and sent to collect the dead from the sick room. Until then I had only seen from a distance the hexagonal plywood sheds used for storing corpses from the camp. I was not sure how many such structures there were. We began transferring the dead from the sick rooms to the storage sheds. There we arranged them in rows, one atop the other. When I went into the "morgue" I was overcome by the awful stench. There were bodies blue from rot! In reply to my question why bodies were collected in piles I was told that Magdeburg Camp could only send bodies to the municipal incinerator once a week. That day I learned a lot about the camp. For example, I found out that the electric current was cut off the fences in the morning and one prisoner was sent to go around the length of the fence, picking off items that had accumulated on it. True, I got better soup that day, but I decided that in the future I would stay away from this work.

That day I also had free time and tried talking with several people who worked in camp services on a permanent basis. I stood by the fence that separated the camp from Rotenza, the worker neighborhood. The houses of the German civilians were very close. It was not like during roll call, which was held early in the morning and towards night when it was getting dark. Now I could see the houses in broad daylight. It was strange to see people living normal lives. I even heard children shouting in the street. Another fence separated the electric fence from the neighborhood, so that the citizens could not be harmed by the electric current. Between the two fences SS men patrolled with their dogs. The second time I walked around the fence the SS man shouted at me to get away. His dog began barking ferociously, it understood well the words of his master, *"Verfluchter Jude"* (accursed Jew). Now the dog was very close to me. His teeth were frightening, reminding me of the punishment roll calls. I fled from there.

I returned to the sick room barracks. Laci, that was the name of the Hungarian, gave me a long look. I thought that he would at least ask me for my name and where I was from. I wanted so much to talk to someone who looked healthy and normal, like people used to be! But Laci was silent, perhaps he did not notice me, as if I was invisible to him. Who was I anyhow? A *häftling, just a* regular prisoner – why would he talk to me? We were the lowest level, while the functionaries, those with jobs who were also prisoners, adapted their behavior to that of the SS, and did not regard us at all. We were not human in their eyes. I thought about this often; had they no shred of humanity left either? Didn't Laci the overseer, for example, think about what would happen when he was liberated and wanted to return to human society? Maybe all the functionaries accepted the Nazi idea that from now on this would be the way of life in the world, and in doing so they really and truly became slaves of the SS?

I realized that the soup was excellent and that it would be

worthwhile to drag the dead bodies, but again decided that the next day I would return to the outside work group. I was more comfortable in the stench of the large group than among the service workers. If Laci did look at me, it was because he heard my question while we were taking the bodies out of the sick rooms. I asked one of the workers what kind of treatment the patients received. He answered that they only got thin soup, so their stomachs wouldn't get upset when they lay on the bunks. "And do they get bread", I asked. "They can no longer chew!", he answered. At that moment Laci passed by and inquired, "Who is asking all the questions?" I became frightened and understood immediately that it would be better to continue my usual routine with the outside work group.

As we walked to work on the industrial zone roads the German civilians never said anything to any of us from the prisoner group, even though hundreds of people passed us going back and forth. Some walked, but most rode bicycles and not once did anyone say a word to us. One day my group stood in place for at least a half-hour because of a railroad barrier. I stood in the last row near, the sidewalk. Nearby stood an SS man. A woman passing by stopped and asked him as she pointed to me, "Do such young boys work in industry?"

"Don't you see there is a red triangle sewn on his shirt?", he replied, "He is an enemy of the Reich!", "Accursed Jew!" She spat on the ground.

Once we had a particularly hard day. It rained slowly and steadily. Even the SS men wrapped themselves in their military overcoats against the annoying rain. What was the point of working today I asked myself. The German civilians took frequent breaks and spent most of the day in the tool shed. We were the only ones outside all the time along with the SS men. Even the *kapos* harassed us less.

I anticipated that after a day like this the evening roll call would be shorter than usual and no one would be punished, especially since I had not seen a *kapo* write down anyone's number. I did not know if other groups worked in places sheltered from rain. I was already soaked to the bone and looked forward to the end of work.

Finally the signal to end came. The *kapos* had us line up in groups to leave for camp. We did not need their goading. We all hurried back to camp. Although we had nothing to change into, we knew from past experience that the clothes would dry out on our bodies. As we stood on the parade ground I felt that everything would go smoothly today. Soon we would get our portion of bread and would be able to wrap ourselves with our blankets and go to sleep.

But after the count, there was unrest on the grounds. The *kapos* sent a messenger to bring the *lagerälteste*, and the count began again, this time more carefully. Every group that was counted was commanded to move a few steps back, to prevent errors. The count continued for more than two hours. It became apparent that one of the prisoners was missing!

The *lagerälteste* rushed to the dog trainer's office and soon returned with the camp commander and the dog. We were afraid. No one believed that someone had escaped. That was impossible! Nothing like that had ever happened, and it was unlikely that it could. I never saw any contact between a German civilian and a prisoner. How could it be then that a prisoner had escaped? That was pure suicide!

I couldn't understand the dog's barks, which were clearly aimed at the SS people, guards and *kapos*. An alarm was set off in the army barracks and a truck full of SS soldiers left the camp. We began whispering among ourselves, discussing various possibilities. One prisoner from the Brabag group, whom I knew only slightly, quietly said that he thought that during the rain someone from the group had gotten under the roof of an abandoned building close to where we were working. He could have fallen asleep there. The regular count after work was done quickly because of the irritating rain, and the SS people were also in a hurry to get back to camp. This, of course, was only a supposition.

The truck with the SS soldiers returned within less than an hour. It turned out that they had found the person, in the factory, asleep. It was already close to midnight. I recalled my earlier anticipation of a short roll call and wrapping myself up in my blanket...

The dog trainer was very anxious. I could not hear what he said, but I saw the group of SS people standing at attention in front of him listening to him berating their irresponsibility. I thought I would soon see how he punished them but that did not happen in our presence.

The "escapee" was put on the punishment grounds. He looked like he had already absorbed quite a few blows on the way back to camp, but the others also wanted to take part in his punishment. There was now a cold wind in addition to the constant rain, and all the groups huddled together against the wind.

"*Achtung!*" (attention), the *lagerälteste* suddenly shouted. "Tonight we are punishing your fellow prisoner because he dared to avoid work and disrupted the good order. We should punish the entire work group, because they were not alert and helped the prisoner slip away".

The prisoner was standing when the dog set on him. The big animal was skilled. The prisoner's screams were not heard at first. In the light of the floodlights aimed at him we saw how the dog slowly tore at his clothes, beginning with his jacket and ending with his pants. After that, the dog began biting, obeying the commands of the camp commander, the dog trainer. The bites were aimed at his arms and the upper part of his body, so he did not fall. Now he began to scream, and my whole body shivered. His howls were animal-like!

Even though it was a dark night, the windows of the civilians opened wide. They already knew what to expect on the punishment grounds, but this evening was special. What were the German civilians thinking? They were certainly glad that the Jews were being finished off, and therefore put up with the interruption to their sleep. Everything for the good of the great Reich! Sometimes during roll calls I would try to distract myself with various thoughts. I would study the buildings opposite me and search for a closed window, behind which Germans would be sitting in shame. But I never saw this; at every roll call all the windows were always open. Those civilians viewed themselves as partners in the difficult war the SS was waging against the Jews on the camp parade grounds.

It was hard to listen to the tortured man on the grounds. Only a choking sound could be heard. Now the prisoner was stretched on the ground while the dog continued his business. The whines grew less frequent, then stopped. The man died. The trainer ordered that the torn body not be removed, so that in the morning we would all see once again what would happen to anyone who disrupted the order.

I don't know how we managed to get to the barracks. As usual, we stood waiting for the portion of bread distributed before going to sleep. Then the Block *kapo* announced that tonight we would not get bread: "Be happy if you get your bread tomorrow. You were all involved in his escape because you kept silent!"

A Jew on the Fence

It rained frequently, and I was worried that I would get sick and that would be the end of me. My shoes were also in bad shape. The soles were completely worn out, and every pebble pained me as I walked. I tried to find out if it was possible to get shoes in the camp. The only alternative was to get wooden shoes with thick wooden soles. I tried fixing my shoes. Like in all camps there was a sewing room and a cobbler shop at Magdeburg for the functionaries who had jobs. An ordinary prisoner was not allowed to go there; only the overseers had the privilege. I was told that there were junior shoe repair workers who would patch a sole for two or three days' worth of bread. Of course I did not agree to this.

Germans carried out *lauskontrolle*[20], lice inspection and control, on rest days, every other Sunday. It was a source of entertainment for the SS men who came in droves to watch the show.

Benches were placed along the assembly grounds. The *kapos* kept order, ordering us to stand on the benches one after the other. We undressed and held our clothes in our hands. We moved forward on the benches to where the SS men were sitting on chairs. The orderly stood opposite the prisoner and commanded him to spread his legs and raise his arms. Body lice were found clustered on every hair, and some stuck to the skin. The number of prisoners with lice was recorded during the inspection, and afterward these prisoners were taken by truck to Magdeburg, since there were no disinfecting arrangements in the camp.

I recall my first trip, which was the first time I saw the city of Magdeburg because from our camp we could see no farther than the Rotenza neighborhood. We now saw many destroyed buildings and boarded-up shops, a testimony to Allied bombing. For the first time since leaving home I saw the signs of war that had reached this area. I felt that perhaps there was hope for a life in the future. We had no idea of how the war was progressing, who was winning or losing. Not even rumors reached the camp. The behavior of the SS men was no indicator, it never changed.

The showers were located outside the city. Apparently the

---

20 *Lauskontrolle* – lice inspection and control.

place was used by other concentration camps since there was a clothing warehouse there. I anticipated that they would surely replace our filthy clothes, but my joy was premature. As I got into the shower I gave my clothes to the prisoner overseeing the disinfecting. The clothes were put into a steam boiler tank for a few minutes. We stood naked and wet until the disinfecting had finished. The clothes were taken out of the tanks and our damp clothes were returned to us, according to our number sewn on the shirt and pants. It was torture to wear the damp clothes, and some lice in the seams survived the disinfecting.

During the return trip I felt completely wretched. Fortunately, it was not cold toward evening and we dried out a little. That night, at the camp elder's speech during roll call, people began coughing which continued throughout the night in the barrack. I hoped I would not get pneumonia, the common disease in the camp.

I learned that many people hid in the barrack and did not report for *lauskontrolle*. Their joy in avoiding the showers was short-lived; their number was recorded and they were forced to go to the next disinfection.

None of the prisoners cared who avoided the inspection and the disinfection. However there were issues to which we were not indifferent, first and foremost stealing bread and the vicious arguments that accompanied its daily distribution. These events led to fist fights, yet the participants' physical condition was so pathetic that the blows petered out to weak shoving, and the two combatants would collapse from fatigue and lie on the ground helplessly. Most of the arguments ended without being resolved. The *kapos* and their helpers never tried to stop an argument between the prisoners. To the contrary, they would encourage them to keep at it, just as they had learned from the SS.

Some of the arguments broke out in the public latrines. In fact, that is where business was transacted. I witnessed many transactions where one side did not keep his end of the bargain. One cigarette sold for a half bowl of soup, for example, but when soup was distributed everyone saw the "debt collector" stand by the prisoner when he got his soup, waiting for him to eat half the portion. Yet the "debtor" did not want to remember the cigarette he had received and quickly swallowed all the soup. Thus the man was left with no soup and no cigarette.

I was happy that I did not need cigarettes. Nevertheless, my curiosity was not satisfied until I discovered how tobacco reached the traders. One day, as we were leaving for work, my neighbor in line begged me to trade places so he could walk on the outside row on the right side. The man walked with his eyes glued to the ground, and when he spotted a cigarette butt on the road or by the sidewalk he quickly bent down and scooped it up. He did this for four kilometers on the way to work. During the soup break he sat in a corner, broke apart the butts and collected the half-burned tobacco into a paper bag. I asked him when he had time to make the cigarettes, and he told me that he was a sort of sub-contractor. Each evening he gave the tobacco to a functionary who always worked in cleaning the camp, and in return he received an extra half-portion of bread every other day. The "collectors" did not always have an easy time of it. During the walk they were kicked plenty of times, both by those walking in back of them who bumped into them and by the SS man, when he saw them bending over by the sidewalk.

Once I told that prisoner that a half-portion of bread was not worth the many blows he got, but he preferred to collect butts rather than buy them with bread.

On a rest day, when I walked by the furthermost barrack in camp, I saw a tall boy sitting on the ground in front of the barrack. I had a strange feeling that I knew him. I stood there staring at him, trying to remember. Finally I identified the freckles on his face: "Aren't you from Miskolc? The city that I am from?" I asked. At first he did not recognize me, but when

I told him my name, he remembered: "You were religious, with *peyes*".

He got up and I saw that he was much taller than I was. I did not recall his name, but after he introduced himself to me as Laci (the same name as the person in Magdeburg camp who oversaw the work) I remembered the details. Here was a boy whom I should have envied back then, because of his comfortable life. His family was well-off, he attended high school, and I never ran into him in the synagogue; in other words his Jewishness was unidentifiable. I remembered that once I had seen him wearing a "Young Maccabi" uniform in Miskolc, and now he told me that he had competed in sports in school and had been an excellent runner.

The boy began to walk back to the barrack with me. I looked at his long thin legs and realized, by the way he walked that he was not in good shape. I told him that today he did not look like an athlete, and he wrinkled his nose and noted that it was a pity that his father had decided not to "make *aliyah*" (immigrate to Israel) when their situation was still good. Of course in his father's eyes, business came first.

"Never mind you with your Zionism", I told him. "I was more disappointed. I was waiting for the Messiah to come. My mother always promised me that when the suffering of the Jews reached its farthest limit, the Messiah would come…".

The boy looked at me in amazement. I think he considered me a little crazy, and perhaps I sounded like it, but judging by his physical condition he looked to me as if he was close to "salvation". He told me he had no one to talk to. All his bunkmates were old, and practically *muselmänner*[21]. I did not tell him that he was so thin that he was not far from that state. I asked him to move to my barrack since there was no list of

---

21 *Muselmänner* - a slang term used to refer to prisoners exhibiting a combination of emaciation and weakness from starvation and an apathetic listlessness, who had lost contact with reality and spent each day rocking back and forth like a Muslim at prayer.

the prisoners in each barrack. I explained that our bunks were sparsely occupied, and every day more space became available as the piles of corpses in the hexagonal sheds continued to grow.

And that is how my friend Laci joined me. We decided to be partners. He brought with him a cloth knapsack where we put our two bowls. I added a soup spoon to the partnership although it was not very useful. We would drink the soup since it was almost never thick enough to eat with a spoon.

My happiness with the partnership did not last long. Laci walked annoyingly slowly. He chewed and ate his bread two or three times during the day, and very often it was stolen before he finished it. So I had an additional worry that I had not anticipated when I befriended him.

Fortunately we did not work in the same group. After roll call Laci would move around sluggishly, not knowing which work group to join. We mostly met in the evening after roll call. I tried to convince him to try harder in order to live, or he would be done for. At night he would complain how difficult everything was for him. I felt a little sorry for him, even though I was hardly better off. My main concern was not to miss my soup or bread portion. The days passed and I could not offer much help to my friend Laci.

One day when we returned from work, as we neared the front gate, I sensed a great deal of tension in the camp. All the SS people stood at attention on the assembly grounds, and the camp commander was also there with his dog. We could not imagine what had happened. I had always hoped that for once they would announce something to cheer me up (even though in my wildest imagination I had no idea what that could be), but I knew from experience that surprises were always harsh. True, before the People of Israel, left Egypt they cried out to the God of Israel and God saved them. But for us salvation was not forthcoming.

Here was Pharaoh in the shape of the dog trainer,

standing on the assembly grounds waiting patiently while the prisoners got into groups. We waited in terrified silence for what was to come. The *Blockälteste* appeared and announced that a prisoner who worked in cleaning the camp had broken into the SS shelter where considerable amounts of camp food were stored. The prisoner had managed to take some potatoes. Until that moment I had not been aware of such a shelter.

"I am telling you that if you do not reveal the name of that prisoner you will stand here until tomorrow morning. There will be no food distribution and you will leave for work in the morning from here!"

We were not surprised. It was not uncommon to stand at roll call for up to four hours, even without pretext of something like stolen potatoes. It seemed that no one knew who the thief was. All the SS men stood patiently while the *kapos* turned in the numbers of those listed for punishment. This was not unusual, but now the dog trainer was present in all his glory. They all wanted to prove their toughness, and the punishments were harder and longer than usual. Many of those punished could not stand up under the blows they received, and collapsed onto the ground. The service workers dragged them all away, but there was still not anything about the thief!

I don't know how long we stood there. The rows became disorganized. People leaned on each other from exhaustion, until they were sitting on the ground. The *kapos* went around with their clubs thrashing them every which way. Even though I was just as tired as everyone, I made an effort to last it out and stay on my feet. I was fearful of the thrashings.

I hoped that the thief would come forward. Obviously the prisoners did not know his identity. If someone did, he would have surely informed on him! The SS people also wanted the ordeal to come to an end. They were there to watch the dog trainer and his "show".

From out of the blue a prisoner was dragged to the front of the grounds and asked "Do you confess?" The man was so surprised he did not utter a word. The dog began jumping around him, tearing pieces of his clothing ever so often. The man's shrieks sounded as if they were from different world. Even though I was fairly callous the shrieks terrified me. The show lasted only a few minutes. When we left the field just the prisoner remained, stretched out on the ground, dead. We did not find out who he was.

The routine of bread distribution and sleep very quickly made us forget these atrocities, horrible as they were. It was very cold at night in the barrack, although it was not yet winter. In the mornings I would see frozen puddles here and there. I don't know if it was the cold or the ongoing starvation that touched off accusations of blanket-stealing during the night. Some people slept with two blankets; others froze from the cold.

The relationship between the prisoners was far from an idyllic comradeship. Each person only looked out for himself. I was so hungry in the mornings that I would turn my pockets inside out, looking for a stray crumb in the seams. I knew that this was an impossibility because I always ate my bread immediately, never keeping it in my pocket. But since I saw the others doing this, I did so too.

We were so exhausted from work and starvation that we did not bother to speak to one another on our bunks. Even the conversations with my friend Laci grew less frequent. In addition to my other troubles I realized that I was not having any effect on him whatsoever. The boy withered away in front of my eyes.

During the walk to work the lice in sensitive places would bother me. I could not scratch and walk at the same time. I also feared that I would open up sores and cause a phlegmonous abscess to develop, a running sore with black circles around it. I damaged my pants when I tore out the pockets to make it easier to scratch, remembering too late that now I could no longer search for bread crumbs in my pockets. Ultimately, the lice were victorious; they continued to bite and burn. There was a reason the SS men avoided getting too close to us.

The days became extremely cold. During the half-hour soup break we would rest huddled together, trying to protect ourselves against the "light" autumn wind as the SS men characterized it. Of course they themselves had warm clothes to wear. We received permission to build a small fire during the break, but it was impossible to have the best of all worlds. When we warmed up a bit the lice would also wake up from the heat, and the party would begin. We would sit around the fire and pull lice out of our armpits, and the adults from their chest hair as well. Somehow there was a gentleman's agreement not to throw live lice: everyone squashed them between their fingernails, which became all red from blood.

This gave the SS men an opportunity to call us all possible indecent names. This was also how I learned to say in German "troublesome swine" or "shitbag". I prayed that the lice would get on them, but like my other prayers this one also went unanswered. Apparently a prisoner could be slapped and kicked, without his attacker getting his lice.

Many times I wondered what more could happen to us. We were already like broken vessels. A few days earlier I heard at roll call that we now numbered 1,300 persons - out of the 2,800 sent to Magdeburg - an impressive German accomplishment in five months. This was not an extermination camp, there were no gas chambers, no firing squads, just a work camp. It was not the Germans' fault that the Jews were weak. I felt like shouting at them, "Devils, I will live!"

One time when we returned from work I saw for the first time a prisoner stuck to the electric fence. Rumor had it that it was suicide. His hands were up against the fence and he could not be identified.

"Here is a Jew who wanted to escape", the *kapos* said.

I did not get fired-up about the sight. I thought that the man had ended his life quicker than in the punishment show.

There were more suicides in the next few days. No wonder, the starvation was intense and our bodies much weaker. Getting up in the morning was grueling. During the morning hours we walked around hunched over, as if to ward off the cold. After the cold and the hard work, the most depressing thing for me was the evening bread distribution. As long as each individual got a portion, it was tolerable. I accepted the fact that sometimes my portion was smaller than what some others received, and I was happy when it was larger. But now the *kapos* changed the system to the one used in Auschwitz. They counted four or five people entering the barrack and gave the last one the whole bread. The ensuing chaos was horrendous. Of course the arguments were bitter, and to prevent them we were forced to conduct a lottery to decide who got which piece. This was cumbersome, and someone with a perverted mind devised a new system to divide up the bread, a scale: a stick with a rope in the middle and nails on each end. Every portion was weighed precisely. I went out of my mind waiting for my portion. No *kapo* interfered with the weighing. If the Jews wanted to make life even more difficult, why should they meddle?

Shoes

I did not know how I looked by now. I felt that something would have to change or I would not be able to carry on. Whenever I looked at my bunkmates I noticed that most of them were not focused, they did not understand what was said to them, and they had lost all human attributes. I noticed people falling asleep while standing as they waited for the cursed portion of bread. Was this the end of the road for us? A terrible fear would seize me when I remembered how the unfit for work were selected at Auschwitz.

Half the people in our barrack were not fit to go to work. Many would fall asleep while standing at morning roll call. Only the *kapo* beatings would get them going. Difficulties at work also worsened daily. Relations between the old and the young were shameful. When we had to carry iron beams on our shoulders the adults did not pitch in, and the young ones had to do it all on their own. They said we had to "respect" them because of their age. They did not get away with it; we avoided working with the older men.

Around this time my friend Laci's condition worsened. He was barely surviving. When I encountered him in a work group at the factory I could not understand what kept him alive. I observed that sometimes he did not get into the bread line. He told me that he simply did not have the strength to stand in line. "I'll sit down and rest instead", he would say. He did not listen to me. I felt as if I was talking to myself. People would ask me why I dragged him along with me. It was hard to explain, but my desire to help him probably stemmed from the fact that he reminded me of home.

Now my shoes were completely worn out. I began to reinforce them with string; it was still better than wooden shoes. On several occasions camp functionaries had asked to buy my shoes, but I always refused. My shoes attracted them because the upper part looked good, and of course they could ask the camp cobbler shop to fix the soles.

I finally made a deal. I sold the shoes to a cook's assistant. He promised to give me an extra bowl of soup every day for at least a month! I readily agreed. Laci, who was present at the deal, registered no sign of happiness even though he stood to gain from it. He was indifferent to everything. In the following days I gave my friend Laci my extra bowl of soup so he would not have to stand in line. His condition improved slightly,, but I saw the indifference on his face and I knew that he would not last much longer.

In exchange for my leather shoes I also received a pair of shoes with wooden soles, like the ones most of the prisoners had. Walking in wooden shoes was tormenting for me. It was very hard to get used to walking in them. Everyone assured me that I would adjust. Some people had been walking in them for many months, so I got used to the situation.

The Cabbage Thief

On one of the Sunday rest days I searched for a family I had met at the camp. The whole camp envied these three people who comprised almost a complete family: a father and his two sons, truly wondrous! I could not understand how these three managed to look so well compared to the others. That Sunday all the camp residents were together. I was surprised that I did not see the three. I began to inquire about their welfare. I did not know their name, but everyone called them "the butcher and his sons". The father must have been a butcher before the war.

I finally met a prisoner who told me that the three of them had worked in the same work group, which was very much to their detriment. The man, who worked in their group, saw one of the sons being slapped by a *kapo*. The father and the other brother defended him and the *kapos* would not forgive them for that. Within minutes the three were done in with murderous blows.

"If you want to see them", the man said ironically, "you can probably still find them in the hexagonal sheds".

The days grew shorter, the nights grew longer, and so did the evening lineups. Every count was conducted out loud, so that the *blockälteste* could hear the final results from where he was standing. I did not track the count results, but the sparseness of inhabitants in the barracks was definitely visible. There was talk among the prisoners that the Russians were advancing on the eastern front. As these rumors became more prevalent, the SS men became more violent.

A new phenomenon developed in the barracks. The stronger prisoners began to dominate the weaker ones. During soup distribution I saw the former pushing to get into line twice, and no one dared object. This even took a turn for the worse as the prisoners began to provoke each other according to their country of origin. The lowest point of all in my eyes was when bunkmates began to denounce each other. There was a large group of prisoners from the Carpathians (Slovakia). They spoke Yiddish and broken Hungarian. Since I spoke Yiddish very well I was not harmed by the rivalry between them and the Hungarians, despite the daily clashes. I liked the people from the Carpathians, and not only because my father was born there. They were stronger than the other prisoners and I considered that a sign of a steadfast spirit. Their toughness enthralled me, and physically they were my role models. I became friendly with several of them. Even Laci, sunk in ceaseless apathy, asked me why I allied with them.

There were quite a few clashes between the Hungarians and the Poles. The *kapos*, who were mostly German criminal prisoners, did not understand the reason for the arguments: "They are all stinking Jews, and good riddance that Germany got rid of them!" they would say. Of course no one asked them, members of the "pure race", why they were in a concentration camp.

All of this was marginal compared to the deplorable state

of our health . One time, when I went to the clinic to request paper bandages, I noticed a large container on the shelf with little yellow pills. I asked what the pills were for and was told that they were vitamin C pills to prevent tooth loss. I showed the orderly my bleeding gums, but he told me that there were more important people there than me. The only thing he was willing to give me was a spoonful of charcoal powder against diarrhea. Like most of the prisoners I suffered from constant diarrhea. I knew one thing for sure: whoever stood in line at the clinic was sure to get that charcoal powder. Many people with diarrhea were very run-down. From afar I could see them walking slowly, their faces smeared with the black charcoal powder.

The weak ones would get pushed around by everyone else for no reason. It was a common sight to see functionaries standing around a prisoner who had collapsed, mocking him for not being able to get up without help. I got so used to seeing this that it no longer bothered me. I needed to look out for myself, only myself! When I saw these prisoners struggling to get up all I could think of was my hope that I would not reach this stage.

I was sure that the SS men only cared about one thing: how to surprise the Jews. And they always succeeded. One evening, when we had been standing in roll call to be counted for at least two hours, I suddenly saw functionaries enter the barracks and drag out all kinds of items: improvised knives, pieces of blanket (used for padding hats) and rusty bowls - no end of items. All the articles were brought to the field where the show began: "You will not be dismissed until the owners of these items come forward".

I was convinced there was no way to identify the owners of these items since they could have come from any of the bunks. It was an attempt to put on a "show" for the SS men, who looked forward to it. Since the punishment lineup that evening had ended, we assumed that this time there would not be additional punishments. They simply left us standing in the lineup on the field, along with several SS men, until the middle of the night. Then they distributed the bread. No one would go to sleep; it was too near the time for morning lineup. I was somewhat surprised that they did not react to the scraps of blankets found in the barrack, since the blankets were the property of the Reich! I assumed the "show" had been postponed until later.

It rained more frequently and the walk to work was even more onerous than before. We would reach work completely soaked, the cold penetrating our wet clothes, making us shiver. During this difficult time I was lucky to find work carrying bricks, thus avoiding having to carry wooden boards or iron girders, work which involved groups of two or three people. I wanted to work alone so I could be free to move. That way I had a better chance of warming up and drying out my clothes a bit. At times such as these I was able to block the present from my thoughts, dwelling instead on the past or the future. I thought a great deal about our family customs when we were still at home. I would concentrate on one of the holidays, the High Holidays or Passover for example, and think only of the food for that holiday. I would think of the menu very systematically, and that way I was able to make it through one more day intact.

During those rainy days I would sometimes find a piece of cabbage or another vegetable in the field surrounding the factory. This would happen in the course of an air raid alarm warning of Allied bombing. All the prisoners would leave the factory and head for the fields. The SS guards, themselves frightened, would urge us to get out of the factory area as fast as we could. In the ensuing confusion we would wait in the field for the all-clear siren.

One day a surprise awaited us: a prisoner had brought a whole cabbage from the field back to camp. The guards noticed it immediately. No one said anything until the lineup for roll call. The prisoner with the cabbage was put in front of the grounds, and we knew that we were in for a hard evening. Of course the camp commander, the "dog trainer", was called. He also stood and waited patiently until the count was completed. We were all tense in anticipation for what was to come. Despite the considerable experience we had with the punishment lineup, there was always a "surprise" during the procedure.

The count was over and the cabbage thief was brought to the open space. Now I could see that the cabbage was huge, at least the size of a human head. While we waited for what was to come I thought that at least four people could have made a meal of that cabbage.

His fate became clear: the entire cabbage would be his. The camp commander ordered him to begin eating the cabbage. As he began to eat many of us felt jealous of the unexpected meal he was getting. The SS men had prior experience with this kind of feeding. All the high-level officers stood in a circle around the prisoner, watching.

His feasting proceeded slowly; he had been eating for about an hour by now. At times he would try to take a break, but of course that was not allowed. The SS man would lay his club on the prisoner's shoulder and he would resume eating. The eating grew increasingly slower and the prisoner tried vomiting. He had not even finished half the cabbage. Now we understood exactly what was going to happen. The show excited the SS men who would roar and laugh when he tried to take a break, "Look, the Jew is full already!"

Then the dog trainer pushed aside the SS man with his stick, drawing closer along with his dog. The prisoner bit off two bites but could not swallow them, and the dog trainer set his dog on him. The dog slowly bit into every part of the wretched man's body. Soon no identifying features were left of him, with wounds over his entire body and the cabbage still in his hand. I did not hear the trainer give the command, but I did see the dog lunge at the prisoner's groin. Within a few seconds he was sprawled on the ground, lifeless.

The "show" concluded with a short speech, "lest we dare steal cabbage from German fields", and the evening ended. It was very late. I asked myself why they didn't just shoot us and be finished with it. Apparently the entire episode followed some kind of German logic. The commander would not contradict his own words, spoken when we came to Camp Magdeburg: "This is not an extermination camp; there are no gas chambers or firing squads here. We are a German work camp." But what was done that night was of course permissible, according to their perverted logic. The man had disobeyed a command: "prohibiting the theft of cabbage", and as the thief he therefore "had to be punished".

Following that event a new arrangement was put into action in camp. When we returned from work our clothes would be searched before we entered the camp gate. It was hard to conceal anything in a pocket and it would be easy to notice from afar. However, the desire to eat was stronger than any threat, and almost every evening someone who had not learned the "cabbage lesson" was caught. The punishment was less sensational than the first "spectacle", and the prisoners who risked stuffing rotten vegetables into their pockets (everything rotted in the fields because of the heavy rain) were punished without lineups and fanfare. Few survived the search and the punishment.

5.

Food!

The cold began to take its toll on us. The number of prisoners found dead on the bunks in the morning continued to grow. This meant additional work for the *kapos* in the morning. The roll call did not match the numbers and they began to look for the missing inside the barracks. We were awakened earlier so we had enough time to bring those who had died during the night out to the morning lineup. As usual, we began to complain about the lengthy lineups that drained us of the little strength we had saved up during the night. As a result each day we left for work in worse shape than the day before.

The violence of the stronger prisoners also grew worse. Stealing bread during the distribution was more common since the weaker prisoners were unable to protect their portions. No one knew how it all began, but a new custom took hold. In the evening, after bread distribution, someone would shout "My bread was stolen!" Nothing more was needed. The Block workers and the *blockälteste* would appear and demand that the victim point out the thief who had taken his bread. To me it seemed impossible to know for sure who the perpetrator was, other than it had to be one of the stronger prisoners. But the victim often pointed to someone weak. I would usually move away and go directly to my bunk, afraid of the violence. However once in a while I was present at this new "show", as someone would point to a prisoner and cry out, "There's the thief!"

The pleas of the accused "thief" got him nowhere. The functionaries would tie him to a beam in the barrack and beat him. The *kapo* would shout, "Whoever had his bread stolen come pay him back!" The following morning his body would be removed from the beam.

I seldom thought about my father. Hunger preoccupied me so thoroughly that I usually forgot anything that had existed before Magdeburg. I did however remember one thing about my father, his advice: "Protect yourself from the beatings", don't call attention to yourself, the less they see you the better off you will be." I made it a habit never to stand at the front of the lineup, and not to be in the vicinity of the *kapos* and their servants.

At Brabag they began to build bunkers as shelters from the bombing. Every morning at the lineup for the group leaving for Brabag, the largest work group, anyone the Germans considered capable of working at pouring cement, including me, was counted separately. I was concerned that I would not be able to do the work but, welcomed the change of fortune.

When we reached the cement pouring area we were assigned various jobs. Some were instructed to fill the cement mixer with gravel and sand, and others to lift the bags of cement. I was chosen to bring the bags of cement. It took me a day to figure out that it was easier to carry the bag of cement than to lift and empty it into the mixer. Freight cars loaded with the cement bags stood about two hundred meters from the bunker. We would line up in a row, each would get a bag on his back and carry it to the cement pouring area. Fifty of us were bag carriers. The first time I went to pick up a bag from the freight car I found that the car floor was the height of my shoulder. Thus I got the bag directly on my neck and shoulders, not on my back. On this occasion the fact that I was short, the same height as the train car floor, was an advantage… Within a few days I learned to keep the bag from slipping off my shoulders and reach the destination safely.

The SS men stood all along the way, prodding the bag

carriers to hurry. People would very often tire and the bag would slip off their back. Some of the prisoners intentionally bent over as they carried the cement, afraid to drop the bag and get kicked by the guards along the way. In the following days many avoided the Brabag cement group at morning lineup. Indeed the work was very hard, my feet were swollen from walking with cement bags on my back and I was very cold. More SS men were added to the Brabag group because of the distances inside the factory. Among the new ones was a German who was older than the others. I noticed that he was also tired towards the end of the walk to work. One morning, when it was less cold on the way to work, the SS man took off his overcoat. I saw him searching the prisoners until he spotted me and said, "*Du kleiner!*" (Little One), as I was called a few times by SS men: "Hold my coat until we reach the factory!"

On top of everything I now had something new to worry about. I took care so the coat would not fall out of my arms. I rejoiced secretly; hopefully the lice would get into the SS man's coat! But in the cold there was no chance that a louse would leave a warm and comfortable place like my armpit or crotch…

After I had carried his coat for several mornings I was in for a surprise. While handing me his coat the SS man pushed a paper package into my hand. I did not dare hope for anything from the little package, but after feeling it I discovered that it had dry bread crusts! (The SS man collected the crusts over several days, perhaps because he had dental problems). The man motioned to me to eat them while walking. This was life-restoring! During the four-kilometer walk to the factory I would take a piece of crust and keep it in my mouth until it softened. After it became soft I would swallow it… How could I not be happy? This happened two or three times, but then the SS man was transferred to a different group.

The Coat

The rain and the cold were intolerable. Someone at the cement pouring site had an idea that we all quickly adopted. We would cut three holes in an empty cement bag and wear it under our shirt. It made a big difference. We were less cold, especially while walking back to camp at the end of a day's work.

It was unclear who informed the guards of this practice. At any rate, after several days the *kapos* began to slap us on the back when we reached the camp entrance . If the sound of a rustling bag could be heard then that person was immediately undressed and the bag taken from him, "for the sake of camp cleanliness". There was another disadvantage to the cement bags: they were useful against the cold but after a few days the cement powder covered our body. We were not clean to begin with, but after wearing a bag I itched all over and had another reason to scratch, aside from the lice.

I met my friend Laci occasionally. His condition was horrendous beyond belief. He got work inside the camp. He washed out the barracks with a rubber hose and picked up trash. As for myself I was far from being clean, but sometimes I managed to wash my feet (without soap of course, we had no such thing). I noticed that Laci smelled worse than me. I told him, "You are in camp all day. Can't you take care of yourself?"

He replied that he had no desire to eat his daily bread, and that sometimes it was stolen from his knapsack. I could not help him.

In the evening I remembered how I had preached to Laci about his dirty feet and decided to do something about the cement powder in my underpants. There was no soap to wash them, but at least the cement powder could be washed out. And that is what I did. At bedtime I undressed, took my underpants to the faucet and washed them out the best I could.

The prisoners stood around watching me, but no one said a word. There were hardly ever any conversations between us.

Before going to sleep I took the precaution of tying the washed underpants to my legs. Since I was sleeping on the top bunk, I hoped that they would dry out by morning, but if not, I would guard them and dry them out the next day. When I got up the next morning I found to my great surprise that only the laces were tied to my legs. The underpants were gone!

I hurried to the lineup. There was no point in searching for the underpants. Someone was walking around wearing two pairs. It was freezing cold. I could not imagine how I would get through the approaching winter. It was already very cold, especially early in the morning. So now I had another new concern. How would I get another pair of underpants? I did not dare report the theft to the *kapo*. He was German, and even though he was a criminal prisoner he bullied us, bragging that he was German and not a filthy Jew.

I was preoccupied with the underpants issue for a long time. There was however one advantage now: without underpants it was easier to scratch when the lice woke up from their daily nap and moved around my poor body. One of the *kapos* once said, "If the lice are alive, it's a sign that the Jews still have enough blood!" Apparently he was right.

During one of the Sunday rest days I saw the person in charge of the sick rooms, the sewing room and the shoe repair shop (which were only for the SS and functionaries). His name was Laci, same as my friend, and he was also from Hungary. I observed him carefully. He appeared to be very healthy! His clothes looked clean and pressed and he wore eyeglasses with broad brown frames. If not for his striped prisoner uniform I could imagine him as the owner of a large enterprise. I decided to approach him to ask for a pair of underpants from the sick rooms. People died there every day, there was sure to be something that fit me.

I gathered courage and went up to him. He must have

been in a good mood as he answered, "I cannot supply you with underpants. Most of them are worn out and we burn them because of the lice. On the other hand, I have here a long coat made of thick material, with a lining. Very few people in camp have coats like this".

It was true that very few people wore civilian clothes over their striped prisoner uniforms. I did not get into the reasons. Winter was approaching and I was willing to do a lot for a coat like that.

"Sir" I said, "I am ready to do any work you give me!" He told me to remain in camp the next morning and report to his room near the sick rooms. Just thinking about the next day gave me pleasure.

The next morning after the lineup I reported to the sick rooms. I was appalled to see the change that had taken place since I had visited there out of curiosity several weeks before. The rooms were now filled with patients. Most of them lay on the bunks without moving, looking lifeless. I identified several prisoners from our work Brabag work group who were there because of severe wounds caused during work.

This was a charade, I thought to myself. The patients did not receive treatment, and were not given bread with the excuse that sick people cannot chew. They were given only soup and coffee. The more experienced prisoners had good reason to advise their friends not to go there for treatment.

I met with Laci the overseer after observing the place for a long time. I wondered what kind of work awaited me here. There were plenty of haulers in the sick rooms. I had once done the work of taking corpses to the hexagonal storage shacks. And no cleaning was done here. After the haulers had removed the corpses Laci called me to follow him. He had a list of identification numbers and he led me to a storage shack. The place did not smell as bad as it did the last time I was here. Perhaps I had become accustomed to the stench of rotting?

Standing beside a pile of corpses Mister Laci pulled a pair of pliers out of his pocket and handed them to me.

"You see that body on the top row? Take the pliers and open his mouth. You will find a gold crown in his upper jaw. What you have to do is to pull the crown out of his mouth. Don't worry, he won't move anymore".

The truth was that I was rather calm. Corpses were a daily sight. The only thing that bothered me was that I had to hold the dead man's jaw open with one hand so I could pull out his tooth. I got the job done quickly.

"Perhaps one day you will be a dentist, if you make it through Magdeburg alive!", Mister Laci joked.

Up until now I had never touched a dead person. Somehow I held his lips open, but my fingers sank into the flesh of his jaw, and the marks of my fingers that remained on the dead man's face looked like fingerprints in clay. Mister Laci stood to the side holding a big white handkerchief to collect the gold crowns. That day I removed crowns and gold bridges from three bodies. As we left Mister Laci wrapped up the handkerchief with the loot, pulled a small bottle of alcohol out of his pocket and wiped his hands.

"Perhaps I could wipe my hands with alcohol too?", I asked.

"You are already so filthy it would not make any difference if you washed your hands or not!"

So far I was satisfied. I received a piece of bread, and he told me to come back at noon to get a bowl of soup!

I followed this routine for several days. I reasoned that if not me, someone else would be found to do this work. Sometimes I asked myself if just patients with gold teeth had died. Perhaps those with gold teeth were selected, beaten to death, and that was that, the loot was there.

I was free for the remainder of the day after extracting the teeth, and I had already received the coat. I was enthralled by its wonderful warmth. Why should I be preoccupied with who had died and who had gold teeth? I already understood something as I noticed that Laci the Overseer was always in the company of *kapos* and SS men in camp. I was not naive. I knew that the SS men sold the gold. The entire camp was under their control, and who would even consider talking about this? It was too dangerous for regular prisoners to talk to them. With the exception of contact with *kapos* in order to carry out their commands, I did not dare look at the SS men as I passed them on the camp paths.

One day I encountered my friend Laci again. He was walking around the camp with some others in a similar condition. His situation was indeed awful. He could barely speak. Laci was almost a *muselmänn*, and no longer went out to work. I asked him if he worked in the camp, but he did not answer. I understood from his stammering that he no longer had the strength to stand in line for soup at noon. Only then did I understand that those who lay in the barracks were no longer hungry. I saw how they chewed on their bread staring off into space... For a minute I was stunned by the deteriorated condition of my friend Laci. I had tried to help him; I had traded my leather shoes for his sake. That had been a bad investment! I suggested that he wear my coat during the day, but he refused, saying he was not cold. That was a crazy suggestion: if he had agreed, someone stronger than him would have taken the coat right off his back!

Towards the end of the week, during roll call, the camp commander brought new tidings: "Whoever feels weak and was unable to work should form a separate group. There were several openings at a rest home near the city. Whoever cannot work will be transferred to a rest home!"

Very few prisoners volunteered. The SS men went through the rows in the lineup and selected the weak-looking. My friend Laci did not heed my warning and volunteered to join the group. I told him that the whole "rest home" story was a lie. Although I did not know where they were being taken, I knew that was the end of him.

The group disappeared, and none of us knew where they were taken. They never came back to Magdeburg. Life continued as before.

I did my new work for several days, but wanted very much to be done with it. I found it very difficult to walk around the camp seeing the *muselmänner*, whose ranks grew from day to day.

I was not sure how Laci, the overseer, would react if I decided to rejoin the work group. Was it conceivable that he would take back the coat? It was so warm thanks to its woven cotton-batting lining. No, it would not be reasonable for him to do that I thought. And that made me feel better.

The final decision to leave came the next day, while making the daily rounds with Laci the overseer. I identified a fresh corpse in the shack, someone who had apparently been brought in the previous day. I knew the man. I found it hard to grasp that he had died so quickly, since a week ago I had seen him at work at Brabag! The injuries on his body gave me a clear explanation of the reason for his death. In the evening I asked Laci the overseer if he had any objections to my return to my work group. I explained that I had friends there and needed to be with them. My apprehensions were unfounded. Laci released me without any problems.

Winter had begun. It had not yet started to snow, but the nights were very cold. In the morning lineup I could see frozen puddles around the camp and I was concerned about what lay ahead. I already had a coat that would keep me very warm, but the general situation in the work group was dire: the prisoners were weaker, the kicking was more frequent, and the only reaction of the German civilians was to demand "stronger prisoners".

The next rest day I considered volunteering for the night shift the coming week. I noticed that those in the night shift group, who returned from work as we were leaving, looked as if they were in better shape than us. They also told me that when they returned to camp they got something to drink before going to sleep. Also, since the night shift group was not large they had plenty of blankets on the bunks. Even though they were sometimes woken during the day to do special jobs, the idea of joining them seemed appealing.

I made inquiries about the night shift work. I got friendly with two or three prisoners who were about my age. I was generous to them, cutting pieces out of the lining of my coat so they could make a kind of muffler to warm their neck. I was afraid the whole coat would come apart so I stopped doing this.

Towards evening I reported to the night shift. The *kapo* in charge did not ask questions. I think he did not recognize anyone and it made no difference to him who was in his group. My new friends advised me which group to join. Only two groups worked at night: one poured cement at Brabag, where I had been working and where the pouring continued day and night, and the second worked at the Elbe River, loading sand brought to where the cement was poured. I chose the second group.

The place appealed to me, as did the group which had only thirty people compared to the utter confusion in the large groups. The group was called the *"Lure Gruppe"* (Lure Group). I observed the work routine by the light of the floodlights. There was a big bulldozer with an enormous arm on the riverbank. The group positioned itself on both sides of a narrow rail that led to the factory. From a distance I saw a small locomotive pulling a string of triangular-shaped hopper cars. The locomotive came to a stop opposite the bulldozer and we all lined up on both sides of the cars, nicknamed *"lure"*. We each had a shovel. The bulldozer driver would pick up a load of sand from the riverbank with the bulldozer bucket and position it above the car. Then we would hold the bucket on both sides with our shovels and the driver would release the sand. He then lifted the bulldozer arm to load more sand. I was satisfied. Although at first I had trouble controlling the shovel when I held it up high, I caught on quickly. Whenever some sand spilled out beside the car, we would shovel it back in.

There was a break at midnight, and our soup portions were brought from the factory. It was quiet and I was glad I had thought of joining this group and did not have to deal with the clamor of a large group.

The nights were cold. The SS men had a tent where they could rest after distributing the soup. We usually did not see the bulldozer driver during the break. Apparently he ate his meal beside the large piece of equipment he operated. One night it was particularly cold. Toward morning there was frost and we were sure we would freeze if we did not jump up and down, a tiring activity, but better than freezing to death. The SS men lit a small fire in their tent. Without asking permission we slowly got closer to the tent. The guard with us on the outside also wanted to warm up by the fire, so he didn't object to all of us going in. One SS man complained nonstop about the stench of the Jews, but we were used to that. We crowded silently around the little fire.

I don't know how it happened, perhaps I was pushed too close to the fire. My coat caught on fire and in seconds it was up in flames! I managed to take it off quickly with the help of the others. It seemed to me that no one else was sorry about the loss of my jealousy-provoking coat. Now I was back to being like everyone else. I thought about all the teeth I had pulled to get the coat, but I soon reconciled myself to the loss. There was no point complaining, and at least I still had a cotton-batting scarf for my neck!

I continued working in the *Lure Gruppe* because of the special conditions in the night shift: I was exempt from the lengthy lineups at camp, the work was routine and most of the prisoners did not cause trouble. We all made an effort to get through the night without clashing with the SS men, even though there was one who was hard to please. We were told that he was from Alsace-Lorraine and we had difficulty understanding his German. He used that as a pretext to punish us. The other guards agreed to let us sit in a corner of the tent during breaks, but the "Alsatian" made every effort to keep us out. He would break wind to make the tent smell and then complain, "the Jews stink; get them out of here!" The other guards did not intervene, and we were forced to sit outside in the cold.

Some people left the Brabag cement-pouring group to join the *Lure Gruppe*, because the work was slightly easier, and only the harassment of the SS man from Alsace spoiled the night for us. I found it interesting that we never saw the civilian bulldozer operator up close. He sat up above in his seat all night, coming down for the food break. When we were in the tent with the SS men I overheard them talking about him between them. They called him *zaufer*, boozer. On the nights when he was drunk he would open the bucket of sand above us instead of above the railroad car. He would release the damp sand on those standing around the *lure* and we had to collect the sand with our shovels and load it into the car. The SS men thought this was funny, as it relieved their boredom.

I do not know whether it was his drunkenness or the desire to abuse us that led him to develop a new technique to frighten us. After opening the bucket and releasing the sand into the car he would pretend to forget to raise the arm back up, returning it to the riverbank in the lowered position. We would all scramble to duck low to avoid being hit.

I stayed with the *Lure Gruppe* for quite a while. Turnover was high and just a few of those who were in the group when I joined were still there. At the same time there were others who wanted to work in this small group. If it weren't for the pestering from the "Alsatian" I would have stayed on. But at the height of winter I decided to go back to the Brabag group.

A Visit from the Red Cross

I went back to sleeping in the camp at night. It had not snowed yet, but the nights were freezing. One blanket did not shield me from the cold in the barrack. Not a night went by without terrible shouts from prisoners whose blanket was stolen while they slept. The squabbles continued throughout the night, with no intervention from the *blockälteste* and his servants. Towards morning all the blankets would be back where they belonged. The lack of underpants continued to torment me. At night I would wake up from the frigid cold and rub my body to keep from freezing.

Work at Brabag continued as usual. I envied the winter clothes of the Germans and the SS men. The prisoners' clothes were thin, no match for the penetrating cold. Sometimes I took off the cotton batting scarf, trying to pick the lice out from their warm home there. The one advantage of winter was that the lice were relatively dormant in their warm abode in my clothes, and I did not have to endure the endless itching of summer.

When working at pouring cement I was close to the refinery part of the plant. I quickly got used to the strong smell of fuel. During the breaks between the cement pouring we would warm by the steam pipes, some of them concentrated in open sheds not far from us. We discovered that every cluster of pipes had pressure valves for releasing steam, and that they leaked hot water. We fell on them as if discovering a treasure. I also drank the water.

Eventually we were warned by the civilian workers not to drink the water because it contained a small amount of fuel that could cause diarrhea. I was very alarmed by the warning. I recalled the severe diarrhea I had suffered in the summer and decided not to drink the water any more. But most of the people did not heed the warning, and prisoners came from farther away to drink the warm water. Almost everyone in the group, except for me, made it a daily habit to drink the water. The warm water gave them a feeling of fullness that relieved the hunger.

After a few days almost everyone in the group had diarrhea. The run to the latrine began that night. Most did not make it to the latrine, and doubled up against the walls of the barracks along the way. The next day, when the SS men saw the feces in the daylight, the guards in the watchtowers were ordered to turn on the floodlights at night and to direct them at the walls of the camp barracks. The prisoners running to the latrine now also feared that they would be shot.

The situation also affected the walk to work in the morning. No sooner had we left the camp that someone had to run to relieve himself. Up until the diarrhea epidemic had erupted we could leave the line and ask the SS man for permission to jump into the field beside the road. We would pull down our pants, relieve ourselves quickly, and run back to our place in line. But now the SS man did not allow us to get out of line, and many relieved themselves in their pants. It was appalling. By the time we got to the factory they no longer needed to relieve themselves (how much could there be on such small amounts of food?), but one SS man said to another: "Look how the accursed Jews shit so much; it looks like they eat too much!" They could see very well that it was mostly green watery liquid, sometimes with blood.

A long line formed at the clinic in the evening when we returned to camp. The patients asked for a spoon of charcoal powder, although we all knew it did not help. From day to day a growing number of people were so weak they could not leave for work. They stayed in the camps, joining the ranks of the *muselmänner* crawling around the camp all day. I did not dare examine their situation closely, afraid of reaching that stage myself soon.

Since I had stopped drinking the water early on, I only

suffered from diarrhea for a day or two. I saw a spot of blood on my pants, but did not concern myself about it.

One day a rumor spread through the camp that the Red Cross would be coming for a visit. I did not give it much thought; a lot of things were said in the camp that proved to be untrue. Once I heard that we were being moved to a new location. Another time I heard that the bread ration was being increased. Was there any truth to the Red Cross visit? I had always imagined them maintaining order and saving lives. If they came, they would have lots to do at Magdeburg! Perhaps they would rescue us and bring humane conditions? Perhaps they would get me the underpants I desperately needed? Perhaps they would get us a little more thick soup, a little more bread…no! It was impossible to ask for so much, even with my exaggerated imagination. If they came at least they would look at us. They would certainly be astonished to see so many people thin as skeletons wearing ragged clothes.

The evening lineup was held earlier than usual. Tension was high. The rumor proved true: Red Cross people were coming today! We felt as if we had gained renewed energy. There was a world outside of the fence; we were not forgotten. The large delegation arrived. They walked by our field. There would be no punishment lineup today!

The count went faster than usual and everyone stood at attention. Not a sound was heard, not even the whimpering heard at every lineup. All the *kapos* stood by their groups. The camp commander arrived, and what a surprise - this time without his dog! The conversation between the visitors and the camp administration was over. The Red Cross people in their civilian clothes reviewed the first row of the lineup, and returned to their places by the SS men. One Red Cross representative stood in front of the lineup, giving a speech I could not hear well, and what I could hear I did not understand. Suddenly, in perfect German, he asked everyone in the lineup, "*habt ihr hunger?*" (Are you hungry?).

"Habt ihr hunger?" (Are you hungry?)

The entire lineup was silent. Only one voice was heard from among the rows, *"Ich habe hunger!"* (I am hungry).

"Ich habe hunger!"

The camp commander remained coolheaded and turned to one of the *kapos* "Please, record the number of the man who is hungry".

The lineup was over, and only the number of the single man who dared complain of hunger was recorded on the *kapo's* paper. I had no doubt the man was mad!

The delegation dispersed, thinking that Magdeburg was a perfect example of how a concentration camp should be administered. Only one prisoner had said that he was hungry!

At the next punishment lineup the man got what was coming to him, according to Nazis rules. The commander and his dog did not get much satisfaction from the show put on for them with this man. The wretched man simply did not endure the punishment and within a minute was sprawled lifeless on the ground.

The first time temperatures fell below freezing damaged all the shower pipes. Drinking water was not available until the next day when the ice around the pipes melted. We all anticipated the first snowfall. We thought it would be easier to contend with snow than with frost. When the snow came, it did not change much in our lives, except for the fact that it covered the entire camp so that it seemed new and white. We tasted it, regarding it as a new item on our daily menu. Even the piles of shit behind the barracks were covered in snow.

After work I performed an act of bravery. I took off my shirt and rubbed snow over my body. Prisoners gathered around looking at me curiously. I didn't know what I looked like (there was no mirror in the entire camp). I realized that my bones protruded, particularly at the joints, aching when I sat or lay on the bunk, and always when I got up from the bunk. Nonetheless, in the eyes of those watching me while I enjoyed the snow, I was in good physical shape. And then one prisoner said: "*Nu*, of course, that boy has connections with the functionaries in the camp!"

I was not naive at all. It was well known that every *blockälteste* had a personal servant who took care of his needs, among them laundry, cooking and cleaning his room. This prisoner was the *stube-dienst*, the *kapo's* servant. I often envied those youths because of their job in camp. They all looked well-fed, clean and dressed in good clothes. It was common knowledge that they also served the *blockälteste's* pleasure. I had seen similar services performed at Auschwitz and Buchenwald.

Was the lie about me the result of envy? Remarks were often heard in the camp about me and other young prisoners: "You will endure and we will rot!" I knew from experience that age was not the determining factor in the will to continue; I was just as hungry as anyone else. Among us there were those who said plainly that we were obliged to endure. Who knew? Perhaps there was a world outside of Magdeburg; perhaps someday we would tell our story; perhaps through us the world would know that every minute of our lives here was measured and determined by the barbarians of the "superior race"… There were others who did not believe that there was any point in stubbornly clinging to life, and gave in to their bitter fate.

The snow melted within a day, but the freezing weather was worse in the morning when we got up, and the muddy snow froze again. We were impatient for the morning lineup to be over so that we could start walking and warm up a little! Lately we had been getting lukewarm coffee in the morning. I felt that those distributing the coffee were taking their time, deliberately. Why give the Jewish prisoners any pleasure? The coffee wouldn't help them in any case.

Cold irritating rain fell all day long, and streams of water soaked through our clothes. We wore cement bags under our shirts during the day. In the afternoon the rain stopped and the freezing weather set in. While walking back to camp I could feel the wet cement bag as it froze on my body. Nearing the gate, as usual, we helped each other pull the bags off in order to avoid punishment when reaching camp.

Generally I took no interest in the results of the count at evening roll call. I knew that we had already dwindled to less than one thousand men, but I was not concerned. The sparseness in the barracks indicated that more than half the prisoners were no longer here. The *kapos* emptied one barrack and put the evacuees in with us. This did not bother me either. Actually, we liked the overcrowding in the bunks. The single blanket we each had did not protect us from the cold, so we would huddle close together to keep warm. No one complained about the smell coming from the bunks as we slept.

The bombing in the industrial area where we worked became routine. It was amazing to see that the Germans did not desert any plant or factory. Additional prisoners were brought in after every bombing, and everyone renewed their work following the destruction.

Bombs were also falling in the immediate vicinity of our camp. The SS guards just tyrannized us more after every bombing, "Don't worry, we are winning, and we will not leave you alive!", they would tell us arrogantly. Rumors began to circulate that the Germans were being routed to the front. We never heard the exact details. The source of the news was the workplace. In the course of these months I had never heard the prisoners offer any commentary about the situation on any front. As a matter of fact, since winter began our situation was so awful that we did not care what was happening at the front. We had only one desire: to get through one more day without an incident at the camp!

One clear night, when it was freezing cold, the camp was suddenly lit as if it were daylight. We woke up in a panic and ran to the front of the barrack to see what had happened. I had never before seen anything like this at Magdeburg. Except for the older ones among us this was an unfamiliar occurrence.

The flares, as they are called today, were nicknamed "Stalin candles". It was a signal that the Russians, who planned to bomb the area, wanted to avoid hitting the prisoner camp. And that is indeed what happened, there was heavy bombing around the camp, and two SS barracks in the vicinity of our camp were totally destroyed. The flames burned throughout night.

The entire camp got up for morning lineup ahead of time. We stood for several hours until we realized that not one of the SS men had been injured. The lineup for leaving camp was conducted as usual, with the addition of curses and abuse from the SS guards. Most of them had simply entered the camp area when their living quarters were hit and set aflame.

Before the lineup was over a group was selected to remain behind at the camp for cleanup duties. The Germans decided to crowd us together and take over two barracks in the camp that would be used as SS quarters. This did not trouble us; we crowded together in winter anyway. Outside, workmen were brought in to move the electric fence.

The SS men did not let us forget the Allied bombing for a long time. Many times during the work day I would hear, "Our enemies are looking out for the Jews! Don't worry, we'll take care of you all right!"

We gained more enemies, this time the German civilians who worked in the factories. The SS men incited them against us, telling them that it was because of us that their barracks had been bombed. Of course no one spoke up to refute their lies. All we wanted was to get through the day with as little punishment as possible!

In the meantime there was a new problem at work: we could not choose the carriers with whom we worked when we carried the steel beams from place to place. Therefore, there would be two or three older workers in each group of carriers. They would not shoulder their share of the load, either deliberately or due to their physical weakness, and most of the weight would fall on the others. This provoked endless arguments.

"You are young, work harder!", the older ones would say.

But that was not the only source of friction we had with them. For example, during soup distribution the older ones would push to the head of the line claiming, "You are younger, you can wait".

Slowly, without explicitly discussing the issue, a deep hatred developed towards the older prisoners. I admit that I was ashamed of myself but I behaved like the others. I saw that the older ones looked out only for themselves, as did everyone else in camp. Why should I have to make any sacrifice for them? The animosity became part of daily life at Magdeburg. I felt that I was fighting for my life, and I could not change that feeling. Even before this there had not been friendly relations between the prisoners. No one made friends with his neighbor.

Considering this situation it was amazing to hear the conversations that took place between us at night, when we could not fall asleep because of the intense cold in the barrack. I could not identify the voices of those who spoke. The conversations were all about life before the war. No one asked, "Where are you from?", or "What was your name at home?" I was very familiar with the way of life of the Hungarian Jews, but most of the Yiddish speakers were from towns in Poland, and I was not acquainted with how they lived. Most of the experiences they described were new to me. Their stories about Shabbat and the holidays were exactly the same as those of Hungarian religious Jews, but what I heard from them about making a living in the shtetl among the goyim was different. Listening to the stories I even yearned for the hard times during the war, when I still lived with my family. It would have been better to fall asleep rather than listen to their conversations, which usually ended on a note of desperation and dark predictions about the future that awaited most of us.

These conversations were not a daily event. They usually

came after an especially depressing evening roll call. One evening the count went on endlessly, for no apparent reason. A fine rain mixed with snow fell, our clothes were soaked, and we had no energy left to jump in place in order to keep warm. The agony was particularly unbearable that evening. I felt surrounded by desperation. Everyone was swearing; I don't know at whom. In the line in front of me an older man stood with arms outstretched to the sky. I tried to hear his supplications. He mumbled, argued, and pleaded for God's mercy. It was dark and the skies were covered with gloomy black clouds. That night the heavens were closed, his pleas would not be answered.

Three Bowls of Soup

It is impossible to forget Hans, the *kapo* with the black triangle, even for a single day. I do not know what kind of connections he had at Magdeburg, but his treatment of the prisoners was particularly harsh and he would intervene with work groups other than his own. Sometimes we would see him after roll call gathering the *kapos* from all the barracks, inviting them to join him in merrymaking. Sometimes we heard him at night when he returned drunk to his Block, cursing and abusing all the prisoners. One thing was evident: the SS men were also friendly with him. I did not tell anyone in the barrack that when I worked at pulling teeth I saw him secretly conferring with Laci the work overseer, regularly. The thought occurred to me that Hans was involved in the death of many of those whose gold crowns I pulled from their mouths. I had no friend in whom to confide and share my suspicions. I did know that I needed to take care when I was around Hans.

Sometimes, on our way back from work, Hans' group and our group were suddenly ordered to stop on a street in Rotenza, not far from camp. We would stand and wait, not knowing the reason. We would see Hans as he entered a house, accompanied by SS men, for what seemed like a long time. Sometimes we waited an hour or more. When he came out he was also accompanied by SS men. When we finally got to the camp the entire lineup would be waiting for our two groups. The other prisoners would greet us with insults and obscenities, because of our tardiness. I was sure that business deals were carried out in that house in Rotenza, and that the gold crowns were also being traded. I had no other explanation for the daily contact between Hans and Laci the overseer.

On one of the rest days I decided to go back to the night shift and hoped that I would hold up physically. I was simply exhausted from the countless lineups and irregular food distribution in the day shift. The arguments between the prisoners multiplied, and every day was worse than the day before. There was no problem switching to the night shift, and I preferred the Brabag work group rather than loading the railroad cars with the crazy SS person from Alsace.

I met several prisoners who were still in the group since the first time I had worked there. No one asked me why I had returned. The first night, when I arrived at work, I immediately understood that it would be better for me to carry bags of cement from the railroad cars to the construction site. The long line of prisoners who carried the bags consisted of many older people who could not keep up with the pace. Fortunately they were able to rest on the return trip without being noticed. It was difficult to watch as the bags slid off their backs, and they had to practically crawl on all fours to complete the route. Everyone was afraid of losing their bag. When a bag dropped to the ground the SS men would fell on the prisoner who has dropped it. After that treatment we had to carry the prisoner back to camp, two of us taking turns holding him up. Luckily I did not encounter any problems during the shift.

I never counted how many bags I carried until the midnight break. After soup distribution there was always a little left in the enormous container. We would stand and wait to see who would get seconds. The SS men would stand near the container and point out the recipients. One night I must have been very industrious: three SS men insisted that I get seconds:

"Der Kleiner" (the little one), they ordered the *kapo*. Sure enough, I got three additional bowls of soup. While I was still eating the second I grew scared. How could I finish the third one? Of course I was afraid to say no. There was no telling how the SS men would react. They stood beside me until I had finished all three additional bowls. Already I did not feel well. I remembered the prisoner who was forced to eat the cabbage in the punishment lineup. By the end of the shift I had strong stomach pains. I could not throw up because everyone would laugh at me.

Night shift work was hard, and accompanied by the proximity of the SS men and the German citizens. It was however slightly preferable to the day shift, with the confusion, the endless lineups that deprived us of hours of sleep, and the many arguments that broke out during evening bread distribution.

I was not the only one who changed his work place every two weeks. I was always under the illusion that "it was better over there". Two weeks later I went back to the regular day shift.

One evening, the *blockälteste* did not show up for roll call. None of us knew the reason. Not until the end of that week did we learn that he had connections on the outside, and had successfully disappeared! We had a hard time believing the story, all these months we had never heard of anything like this. Some said that he was a Communist with outside connections.

Anyone who thought about this logically did not believe the story. They said it was more likely that the camp commander had gotten rid of him, had him transferred somewhere else. Soon we began to miss him. We recalled that everyone wanted to stand in front of him during the punishment lineup, to be punched by him and his fist. The man knew his stuff. He would do a kind of shoving blow, and the prisoners whom he punished would get up off the ground in one piece with no real damage done.

The winter was harsh, as was the social situation in the barracks. "Doling out justice" to the bread thieves, without interference from the *kapos* or the Germans, became a regular occurrence. The Germans could always claim, "See, the accursed Jews are killing each other!" I was so hungry that I sometimes thought to myself, "It's a good thing that they are taking the law into their own hands. After all, whoever steals bread is stealing life".

And as if to top off our "good life", it was announced that on our next rest day there would be total disinfecting, this time without lice inspection. It was such a cold day that very few people were outdoors in Magdeburg when we were taken to the municipal disinfection station. I was very apprehensive of the outcome and as a matter of fact nothing changed since the last time. Again after the shower I got back my uniform with my number, and again not one louse had disappeared despite the disinfecting. The clothes did remain damp however.

At night I woke with a burning fever. A prisoner put his ear to my chest and claimed to hear rales in my lung. Pneumonia, no doubt! I was afraid to move. I knew what this meant and considered what I should do. My bunkmates advised me to go to the clinic the next day. How naïve they were! I think that I was among the few who knew exactly what my fate would be if I reached the sick room. I did not have a clue what I needed do to get healthy. I recalled that once, before the war, my mother had wrapped me in a wet sheet to bring down my fever when

I was sick. And now I was lying on the bunk, wearing the clothes that were still damp from the disinfecting. Perhaps the dampness would bring my fever down?

I did not take anyone's advice. The next day I went to the morning lineup. Before the lineup they always chased everyone out of the barracks, since the count had to match. After the lineup I managed to get back to the barrack. There were lots of blankets on the bunk since all the prisoners had left for work. I covered myself and decided that no matter what happened, I would not go to the clinic!

During the day many *muselmänner* who did not go to work walked around the camp. Everyone knew that they would die within a few days, so no one checked the barracks during the day. The only disadvantage was that I could not get my daily soup ration. Towards evening I went out and joined the lineup. That way I would at least get the bread. I was in dire need of the soup, but I also knew what I was doing, and I was careful not to make a wrong move.

That is how I got through the week. Finally I felt that I no longer had a fever, but I was very weak and apprehensive about the coming work week. I decided to go back to the night shift, but not to carry the cement bags. Perhaps I could find some other work?

I left the camp with the night shift and got lucky. Because I was short I was assigned what I thought was a lifesaver due to my run-down physical condition. The supervisor of the cement-pouring work was looking for a young person who could climb up to the top of the shelter, which was almost four meters high. The entire shelter was made of poured cement. The top part had not been poured yet and the frame was made of iron mesh construction where the builders had left an opening to the top. The workers were hauling up the cement with an elevator and pouring it into a conduit. My job was to stand in one spot with a long wooden stick and push the poured cement from above so that the flow would not stop.

I was alone at my station. The work was hard but easier than carrying bags of cement, and I got used to it. I wore empty cement bags under my clothes to protect myself from the wind. All parts of the building were lit with floodlights so I could see all around. Suddenly the alarm sounded.

I had been wondering what had happened to the Allied forces lately. There had been no bombing the last few days. During an alarm the routine was to turn the floodlights off and on to warn people to leave the factory. Even though I was already familiar with the passages between the beams, I had a hard time finding my way between them in order to get down. My wooden shoes got caught while I was climbing down and I could not free them. I bent over to get my feet out of the stuck shoes. I managed to get out of them, but severely injured my ankle.

In the meantime everybody had left the factory. I remained lying next to the structure, unable to move my leg!

After the all-clear signal was heard everyone returned to work, but I remained sitting where I was until the end of the shift. I checked my leg and saw that except for the open wound, it was not injured. I found my lost shoes and put them on despite the pain.

In the morning, on the way back to camp, I felt that I lacked the strength to continue. I did not want help walking; I wanted no part of that daily scene of carrying the disabled. I took off my shoes and was able to walk more easily. I managed to make it back to camp on my own despite the difficulties.

Before I went to sleep I tried over and over again to put the shoe on the wounded foot, but finally gave up. Despite my fear and revulsion from the clinic I went there to get help. I knew exactly what the help would be and I was right. The orderly washed my foot with water and gave me a paper bandage to wrap around my ankle. Before going to sleep I wrapped a burlap bag I had found by the storerooms around my foot and tied it tightly. I knew I would not be able to put on a shoe.

At night I went out with the night shift as usual. The bag-bandage made the pain bearable. I experimented with walking and was satisfied with the results. I preferred to work rather than stay in the camp with the sick. I knew very well what the fate of those remaining was: they did not always get fed! Therefore, I chose to go to work under almost any condition.

During work I felt strong itching in the wrapped ankle. When I opened the bag after a few days to see how the foot was doing, I was not surprised to find pus covering the entire ankle. I went to the clinic every day, and asked for a paper bandage. The pus, which I cleaned out myself, turned a bloody gray color.

The pain went away after a few days, but I was worried that the pus would spread. I also saw that other people's wounds did not heal. When prisoners complained about wounded fingers or toes the orderly would cut off the infected limb and thus complete the medical treatment. I slowly became used to my new situation, and once again only the cold and hunger troubled me, along with the single disadvantage of working the night shift - being awakened during the day when there was an urgent task to be performed in camp. This disadvantage sometimes spoiled all the advantages of the night shift.

Two Hunks of Bread

Through my sleep I often heard the alarm that preceded the bombing of the city. This did not usually bother me. One time, the camp workers woke all the prisoners who worked the night shift and took them by truck to Magdeburg.

Hundreds of citizens crowded around the destroyed buildings in the city center, looking for those who had survived. Our job was to help the search. We had a hard time keeping up with them, because of our exhaustion and lack of sleep. The rescue teams tyrannized us mercilessly, and the civilian population took advantage of the opportunity to beat us since we, the Jews, were guilty of the bombing! Our work was accompanied by shouts, shoving and curses *"verfluchte Juden"*(accursed Jews) - this time not from the SS but from ordinary German citizens.

While searching for survivors we tried to find any food in the vicinity of the destroyed kitchens. All we found were some spices, nothing to stave off our hunger. Every two hours there was a break in the search in order to confer with the city engineer. We used the breaks to get some rest. During the breaks the Germans did not forget to keep us in a place farthest from the rubble, to prevent us from looking for food. During these breaks volunteers from local women's organizations passed out warm drinks to the German workers and the SS men who guarded us. We were never given anything. My heart cried out at the evilness of this nation. These women were mothers and wives, and we Jews were looking for their loved ones! How could it be that not only the SS people hated us, but also Germen women and mothers? I promised myself that if I survived, I would also hate the Germans for the rest of my life.

The talk I heard, and the glimmers of hope for a future in which we would continue to live or at least survive in Magdeburg, had no basis in reality. Chances lessened from day to day. I stopped inquiring about the results of the count at lineups, no longer keeping track of the series of events befalling what remained of Magdeburg Jews.

Once again I left the night shift. None of the *kapos* showed any interest in which group I joined, day or night, as long as I went to work and showed up for the count at lineup. I began the day shift on a bad note. I was already used to the work, but seemed to have forgotten what accompanied the evening lineup: the drawn-out anticipation for the end of the lineup and the bread distribution, the overwhelming desire to go to sleep wrapped in my single blanket, trying to find a comfortable position on the bunk and falling asleep.

That day I could see that the lineup would take a long time. I based my guess on the weather. The fine rain mixed with snow was a perfect reason for the *kapos* to draw out the lineup. Usually the worse the weather the longer they stretched out the lineup. They wanted to show their hatred towards us and to find favor with the SS men any way they could. They would arrange themselves in back of the groups, and since they were warmly dressed they could wait quietly for the end of the count.

That night the *kapo* Hans showed up for the lineup in a special mood. Perhaps he had drunk a little medicinal alcohol? He began walking around the groups standing in the lineup. When Hans walked between the rows everyone lowered their heads, as if to make themselves invisible. A blow from his club was fast and usually fatal. Hans just waited for an opportunity to land a blow.

The prisoner beside me moaned out loud. Had he lost his wits? He knew very well that Hans was nearby. Hans turned around with a smile on his face. He had finally found a victim. Quick as lightening his club hit the prisoner's ear. Blood spurted from his ear in a great jet stream. The man did not manage to utter a sound before he collapsed. Hans did not stop there of course, and ordered us to prop the prisoner up on his legs. A minute later he came back to the man, who apparently thought needed some more discipline. Again the damn Jew collapsed silently after the first blow, angering Hans.

I blocked out the scene and tried not to hear anything else. I withdrew into myself, hoping he would not reach me. That devil would turn around suddenly, trying to catch someone looking at him. Everyone knew that it was forbidden for a Jew to look at a German, even if he was a prisoner. Every functionary who was a prisoner was allowed to beat Jews, and a *kapo* certainly could do as he pleased. I always took great care to get through the lineups peacefully. The blow I had received earlier, while the rows were being straightened in the lineup, was enough for me: everything spins around you, and you see only blackness and pray that you will not fall to the ground! They wait to see you lying there; it is easier to end a prisoner's life when he is on the ground. Little damage is caused to the glossy boot.

All things considered, the lineup was not going to end soon. It became evident that they still had surprises up their sleeve. How many more lineups like this would we be able to survive? You in the heavens above, you the "all-powerful", this one time I extend my plea to you. Please, open a narrow crack up there, and listen to Israel! If you are unable to help, at least take me to you.

Amidst all this despair a surprise awaited me. I encountered another youth from my city. I did not actually know him, but in bygone days I had run across him once in a while at the synagogue. I don't know why our paths had not crossed at camp over the past months. This was likely due to our indifference toward the others that characterized our behavior. We did not usually walk around the camp. What was there to find in the other barracks? That said, we did meet.

I convinced him to move to my barrack, and to make a "knapsack pact". Neither one of us had anything to put in the knapsack except for our tin bowls and cups. We became bunkmates. One thing bothered me: the measured way he ate his portion of bread. Every few hours he would eat a few bites and return the bread to the knapsack. I tried to convince him not to do this for fear that it would be stolen. However Yossi (I asked him what his name was much later) maintained that even though his bread sometimes "disappeared", it was worth the enjoyment of eating from it throughout the day. He was among the few who did this at Magdeburg, except for the *muselmänner* who were indifferent to food and barely ate their ration which was often eaten by others.

We became friends. We would talk a lot about our hometown, Miskolc, and how we would go back there. I considered him to be more naïve than me. He reminded me that his father had owned a large metal warehouse and was a rich man. I did not attach much importance to his talk. My imagination did not reach that far into the future. I explained to him the outlook on life I had developed here at Magdeburg.

During the day we were never together. He claimed that he did not have the strength to go to work at Brabag and preferred to remain at the camp doing odd jobs, even though there was no predicting which crazed *kapo* he could encounter. We remained friends and shared the same bunk.

For two nights I could not fall asleep. My whole body was tense and although I was exhausted from the previous day, I still could not fall asleep. Perhaps it was because the past two days I realized that Yossi, my bunkmate and knapsack partner, was drifting away from me. We no longer talked about food, about home or about our longing for times gone by. During the quiet nights at Magdeburg we mostly talked about the size of tomorrow's portion of bread. Would it be big? Would it be half-baked, or maybe crusty and flaky?

I could not fall asleep because something troubled me deeply: why wasn't Yossi, my neighbor and friend, talking? The night was supposedly quiet, but if you were not asleep you could hear things that took place in the dark of the night. The bunks were crowded. Someone rolled over in his sleep, and the person at the end of the bunk fell off and then climbed back to his place. Here and there a weak cry was heard; a man had died in his sleep. Now it was dark. In the morning, at roll call, we would know who he was, and already we would not remember exactly what he looked like. Each one unto himself. Fatigued and weary I finally fell asleep.

Apparently, in my troubled sleep, I had extended my arm and my hand touched something tucked under my neighbor Yossi's blanket. I woke up as if electrified and quietly tried to digest the fact that my fingers had touched two pieces of bread! I extended my hand carefully and again found the exact spot... Yes, now I was absolutely sure, at least two portions of bread!!!

This could not be, I thought. We ate our evening rations together. I ate mine quickly, and my friend, as if to anger me, cut his into little cubes with an improvised knife and left a few for later. But two additional portions of bread? The night went by slowly. I expected that in the morning my friend would tell me where he had gotten the bread. Was he going to keep it another day? Who knew, perhaps we would share it?

Another day went by. We were on the bunk and he had not said a word. I was restless but decided to wait one more day. What would happen if I took some of the bread and he woke up? We would no longer be friends. He would shout "bread thief!", and that would be the end of me. My sentence would be carried out on the spot. The punishment: to be hung on the central beam of the barrack for all to see. Stealing bread meant stealing life. No one would believe me that there had been two rations of bread! While these thoughts raced through my mind, I groped at the bread and let my imagination run wild. As I touched the bread I could see in my mind's eye my parents' home on a Thursday. Throughout my childhood, on Thursday my mother would bake two gigantic loaves of bread for the entire week. The crust was thick and flaky, fragrant, maddening... That night I could actually smell it. No I thought, I was not mistaken. The bread was right at my fingertips, I just had to reach out, and it would be mine. If I decided to take it, I would eat it quietly, slowly, I had all night, I had all night... I was overcome with madness. I would do it, I thought.

I could no longer hold back. I extended my hand, grasped,

and it was in my hand. I lay on my friend with my entire body to keep him from creating a scene. I plugged his mouth and whispered, "If you shout, I will choke you!"

Yossi calmed down. He did not reveal where he had gotten the bread, but he confessed that for two days he had not found an opportunity to be alone with the bread so he could eat it. We spent the rest of the night under the blanket, quietly eating, talking and dreaming, talking and dreaming…

Of life and freedom…

Of weekday bread…

Of *challahs* [22] for Shabbat and holidays…

Of fish and sliced carrots…

Of golden soup with noodles…

Of the dream of surviving!

It was the depth of winter. Snow fell heavily at night. During the day the weather was clear and pleasant, but the days were frightening in the absence of hope or expectations. Returning from work was difficult, especially when the snow melted and we sank in the slush.

I had to take the bag off my wounded leg at night because it was all wet. The wound with the pus began to bother me again. My ankle would swell up at work during the day and on the walk back to camp. Sometimes I would try to wear the wooden shoe on my painful foot. It was not easy to decide what was better: a wet foot in a bag or a shoe pressing on the wound. I was undecided for several days until I trained myself to wear a bigger shoe on the wounded foot and give up the burlap bag. I was mainly afraid of catching a cold again and coming down with pneumonia from the dampness on my foot. The fact that I recovered from the first illness amazed all those who knew I was sick.

A surprise awaited us one evening, courtesy of the

---

[22] *Challah* – traditional Jewish bread, usually braided and typically eaten on ceremonial occasions such as the Sabbath and major Jewish holidays.

prisoner functionaries during their long hours at camp. They combined several barracks and emptied out another. Thus I knew that many prisoners had already "left" Magdeburg. Again we lay crowded together, there was no point complaining. The emptied barrack was far from the center. It was the third barrack to stand empty. The prisoners who came from that barrack claimed that it was easier to sleep there because the *kapos* did not come by very frequently. In contrast, when an argument broke out in one of the central barracks the *kapos* would hear about it, tell others, and everyone would join in the "party."

The month of Kislev [23] 5705 (according to the Jewish calendar)

December 1944.

Hard to know how we knew that.

The very cold weather, the dampness and hunger tortured our souls to the extreme. These were days of desperation, and just the shadow of a spark of life broke through from the underworld. Suddenly most of the prisoners were urgently summoned to the central building. We stood in a crooked line at the entrance, and no one had a clue as to the surprise that awaited us this time. The line pressed together, and no one strayed aside. The frozen snow was melting, and we stood back to back to keep what little warmth there was in our body. Our clothes had been damp for hours and there was no chance to dry out. And now, instead of sleep, we were summoned to a "surprise" in the central building.

We advanced very slowly. From the entrance came calls goading us forward. We entered, one behind the other, and then came the command: "Face the center!"

The crowding was stifling, with damp and nauseating vapors around us, making it hard to breathe with all the stench. I estimated that we had already lost three hours of sleep, and still no sign of the beginning of the "surprise."

---

[23] *Kislev* - the third month of the Jewish calendar.

The entrance area emptied out, and into the cleared space gathered *kapos* from the camp staff, most of them drunk. An accordion player was found, the only one who was not drunk.

We waited patiently, as usual. It seemed that the evening would pass peacefully. Slowly it dawned on us: it was Christmas Eve! All the "guests" sat at the entrance and the *blockälteste* began the evening with songs about Jesus. Suddenly the master of ceremonies stopped and turned to us shouting:

"Cursed Jews! Which one of you is ready to sing in honor of the occasion?"

Quiet. From one corner the sound of movement was heard, and a clear, unidentified voice broke the silence, "*Maoz tzur yeshuati…*", Rock of Ages [24].

This Christmas celebration marked a turning point in my overall state of mind. Rumors spread that the Allied Forces were winning battles against the Germans on all fronts. It was hard to take seriously the crumbs of information that reached our ears. There was no noticeable change in the behavior of the SS towards us, and the *kapos* were harder on us than usual. Once I heard a *kapo* say "Don't worry Jews. Even if the Germans are defeated, you won't be alive to see it".

Such thoughts were not unfounded. The kitchen workers, under SS orders, began diluting our one daily ration of soup. There was little chance of finding anything thick at the bottom of the huge container after it was emptied. We all lived on a bowl of watery soup, a cup of black coffee, and a portion of bread that got smaller and smaller. I would finish my bread immediately, and feel as if nothing was in my stomach. Just the thought that I would have to wait 24 hours for the next portion would drive me crazy.

Our situation only worsened with the rumors of imminent German defeat. At head count I heard that we now numbered

---

[24] "*Maoz tzur yeshuati…*" - Rock of Ages, a song sung during the Jewish holiday Hanukkah, which is celebrated around the time of Christmas.

about 600. The truck that collected corpses now came to the camp more frequently, not just once a week like last summer.

The *kapos* and their helpers in the barracks cooked their meals virtually in public. We would stand outside their rooms and smell the food frying. Once I even asked the *kapo's* servant to let me rinse his master's plate. Of course I was driven away. I was ashamed, I had reached such a low point that I was willing to lick the *kapo's* plate? Let it all be over with!

On the rest day the servants stood and jeered at the prisoner who crawled towards the electrified fence to put an end to his suffering, "Nu, crawl *muselmänner*, finish already!"

I did not expect any sort of humane treatment at Magdeburg. The place was cursed from the beginning! Nonetheless here we were close to the end of the war. Perhaps, at the very least, the prisoner functionaries would agree to treat us a little better? No one asked them for food, they were prisoners just like us! More than once we saw the SS beating the servants as well. The SS men regarded all others as lesser creatures. Most of the *kapos* were appointed by the Germans, not because they were Germans but because they were criminals and tougher than the others.

At night we frequently stood outside the barrack quietly to see the bombing with our own eyes. The bombs did not scare me, even if a bomb fell in the camp the number of those killed would not exceed the usual number of the dead collected at Magdeburg every day.

At the work site I noticed signs of nervousness among the civilian supervisors. There were at least three sirens every day during which everyone left the building. We continued to pour cement as usual, but the number of people in our work groups dwindled. The Germans took their anger out on us. They were furious because of the small number of workers. Even though we worked physically close to the German civilians, it was unusual for a German civilian to converse with a prisoner.

Most of the time all we heard were words urging us to work faster.

I thought a lot about this. If the Germans needed us for work (most of the work at the factories was performed by prisoners), what explanation was there for the inhumane treatment towards us? If they gave us a little more bread they would get more use out of us. I once overheard a supervisor asking the SS why they didn't bring stronger prisoners. Try explaining to them that the purpose of Magdeburg camp was not to house and maintain prisoners; it was a concentration camp run by the SS.

The problems that arose before leaving for work intensified. After morning roll call the *kapos* had a hard time rounding up enough healthy prisoners to fill the work groups. The number leaving for work had to match the number requested by the factories. Therefore, workers who could barely walk were also taken to work. For us it was a grueling additional effort: when leaving for work we already had to support some of the people, and the four-kilometer walk was tiring for the healthy ones as well. We would drag those that needed help to the factory and prop them up against the walls of the buildings as we were ordered by the SS. They would sit there until the end of the work day, to the great anger of the supervisors. Hauling them back to camp was much more difficult.

6.

Back to Buchenwald

The momentous turning point was sudden. No hint or rumor prepared us in advance. Wake-up was earlier than usual and it was totally dark outside. The entire camp area was lit by floodlights. At morning roll call we all remained on the field. We did not understand why work groups were not organized as usual. Some of us were sent to the sick rooms to help evacuate those lying there. There were not many and they were brought out and placed on the field for another count. At the count we found out that only 400 of us were left.

Army trucks came to the camp at dawn, and all of us, including the sick, were loaded onto them. I felt encouraged. While we were being held here prisoners died daily. Perhaps if something were to change more people would remain alive. I did not know where the Germans were taking us, or for what reason, but this thought went through my mind over and over again: I had succeeded in surviving the camp. We had numbered 2,800 when we arrived, only 400 of us were leaving, and I was among them!

We had no way of knowing where we were being taken. The trucks waited until they were loaded, and the convoy then moved in the direction of the train station. I dared ask the *kapo* stationed at the open end of the truck where we were going.

"Where do you think? Where are Jews taken?", he answered.

I was not shaken by his response. I was accustomed to the immense hatred towards us.

The train cars were waiting for us at the station. I already had experience in the kind of journey that lay ahead. We arranged ourselves in rows, each one sitting between the legs of the person in back of him. Nonetheless, there was something different about this journey: two or three times a day the train stopped and the cars waited on a side track, far from any populated area. We were allowed to get off during the wait and could relieve ourselves in the field under the watchful eyes of the guards. Sometimes we had to wait hours until other trains, packed with German soldiers, went by on the main tracks. After they passed our train would be returned to the main line and we would continue on our way.

On the second night of the journey I heard that we were returning to Buchenwald, the camp we belonged to, whatever that meant. I recalled that the trip from Buchenwald to Magdeburg was only a few hours long, and now the return trip was much more complicated. The stops grew longer, we did not travel at night and we slept in the same position in which we sat during the entire day.

I felt bad. The first two days we received bread only once. However we could drink as much as we wanted. All the stops were at train junctions where there were giant water taps, and we were allowed to drink from them. I lost track of time. There were also positive surprises along the way. Large vats of soup awaited us at some stops. However, it was hard to feel full from one portion of soup every two-three days. Still, for us this meant life!

On the second day I found out that the unconscious and the dead were being moved to the car with the sick that had been evacuated from Magdeburg. People who got off to help move the bodies reported that two cars were full of corpses.

The train continued its journey. It was my fourth train trip, but at least this time I knew where I was headed. I thought about the hardships I had endured at Magdeburg. It was strange to contemplate the day we had first arrived there. The camp had been full of people, most of them in reasonable physical condition, and they all went to work. At the time I had been full of fears. I was still traumatized by the selections at Auschwitz and I was sure that at Magdeburg they would decide that I was too young and not suited for work. I was so happy that at this camp no one checked who was fit for work! Now I remembered the butcher and his family, a father and two sons, and how healthy and strong they were compared to me. How alert and sturdy the boys from the Carpathian mountains were, how they knew how to look after themselves, and now most of them were dead: they had been here, and now they were gone! Fate had cheated us all. How had 2,400 people disappeared? No one was shot and no one was put to death in a gas chamber. Just as the camp commander had told us at the "reception" held in our honor when we had arrived at Magdeburg: "this is a work camp!" In the end here I was, one of 400 who had survived. Magdeburg had not killed my spirit; only my body quivered a bit. Everything could be fixed with the help of several slices of bread.

And why were we brought to Magdeburg? To entertain the SS? Perhaps to display us to the pure-race citizens of Germany living near the camp? They did not benefit from us that much. At the lineups the SS men at Magdeburg frequently spoke sarcastically about the Jews, and now I saw that they had "defeated" us, without bullets or gas. I looked around; none of the prisoners looked familiar. It was as if everything that distinguished them and made them individuals had been erased, and all that remained was the number. Living skeletons were traveling with me on the train! No doubt I looked no different. Had I also lost my features? Only the eyes were still alive.

I tried to fall asleep. It was difficult to hold my head up straight and sleep, and the person behind me would not let me lean on him. We had never been so filthy dirty. Here and there

I saw someone mumble something to a friend. The SS guards were nervous. I did not understand why they were sitting with us in the door opening of the train car. Apparently those were the orders they had received, that order had to be maintained even in the train car. They carried out their duties faithfully, even if they had to suffer the stench of the Jews for the sake of the Third Reich. The entire time I was at Magdeburg I had never seen a German soldier show any humaneness when he saw how we were demeaned and dying slowly.

We moved, we stopped, and we waited for hours…the soldiers of the Reich traveled with their firearms. Where to? Certainly in the direction of Berlin, only 80 kilometers from Magdeburg. It looked like the end of the war was approaching. Maybe now, towards the end, things would get better for us? If only we would arrive already! I kept thinking that I had to commit everything to memory, so that I could tell everyone.

We were standing by the cars, standing and waiting. In the daylight fir trees could be seen up to the horizon. It would be interesting to try to eat the tree trunks, but I never tried. The guards were sitting, smoking and talking, certainly not about us. They all had a family back home. They surely corresponded with their wives, writing about their heroic deeds on the Jewish front… Were it not for the need to watch the miserable prisoners, they could have fought at the front and perhaps been victorious. But what could they do? First the Jewish problem had to be taken care of, just as they had wiped out the homosexuals, the mentally ill, and the Gypsies. Perhaps a few Jews would remain, as a museum exhibit?

Again we got back on the train. The track was finally free. Buchenwald, our destination, was not far. Would I soon hear the camp orchestra play in honor of our return, and would we sing the camp hymn: "Buchenwald, I cannot forget you, because you are our homeland"?

A new morning, a new station. We received a bread ration, not large but at least something. No sooner had I started eating and I was already finished. A loud argument broke out in the back of the car. The guards reacted as if they had been waiting for this moment. This was entertainment for the SS men, and this time right in our car! Even though they had already given up the fight, the two sorry prisoners were placed standing opposite each other in the space cleared for them in the car. Their physical condition was run down of course, and neither one was interested in hitting, but "the show must go on". Having no choice they pushed each other and wrestled like two shadows. Even the guards did not find it enjoyable, and perhaps that is why they added a few blows of their own. Finally the two collapsed, sank to the floor, and were pushed into a corner of the car. Would they ever recover?

We arrived at Buchenwald as night was falling. Immediately after getting off the train we stood in formation to be counted. The "anticipated train wagons" arrived and the death commando went into action. They had to empty two cars full of corpses. None of us took a particular interest in this. We waited only for the lineup to come to an end because after it came the bread distribution.

But this was not what happened. We were taken to quarantine for disinfection, which I remembered from the previous time I had arrived here from Auschwitz. The enormous quarantine yard was full of prisoners, and we intermingled among them. I heard that there was a long line for the disinfectant shower, no one worked there at night and we all had to wait until morning. I asked someone about the chances of getting bread or soup, but he did not know. That was what we were all waiting for.

There was a certain order to the place. The group that had arrived before us was from the town of Tzeiz, which was also a sub-camp of Buchenwald. It appeared that we were all being brought back to the main camp, Buchenwald. The Germans were not interested in having the prisoners liberated by the approaching allied forces. Thus they were "saving" us from liberation. They had other plans! Night fell, and we all sat in the yard trying to find a sheltered place to pass the night. I wondered if the next morning we would all get to shower.

Snow began to fall in the morning, and it was easier to bear the cold. We all stamped our feet trying to warm up, after freezing all night without sleep. Prisoners who no longer moved were sprawled in the corners of the yard. Apparently they were finished: they were liberated. I moved among the people in a daze. I did not bother to look for acquaintances. What would acquaintances and small talk help me? There was nothing left to talk about. I saw the end of the road right here in this yard.

The prisoners finally began to go into the showers. There was strict order. Those from the Tzeiz group had arrived before us, and they also went in before us. We continued to wait our turn. The day passed slowly: what a wonder it was that apparently no one had died that day! It was night once again and the showers closed, and we were still on the outside. Twenty-four hours had gone by and we were still in the quarantine yard. At night we crowded together trying to sleep close to each other, to protect ourselves from the harsh cold night. Perhaps I won't sit with all of them? Perhaps I will walk around all night? No one dies standing! However I did not feel that I was at the finish line. I spent most of the night walking around the yard. At some point I fell asleep in a far corner, awakened by the morning wind.

The snow was deep, and only the path to the showers was packed down by those who had passed through the previous day. Additional corpses were piled up. Apparently it was easier to die together. Here and there I saw someone get up from the pile and shake himself out in preparation for a new day. It was impossible to count the bodies. I did not know how many of them were from Magdeburg. No one asked; no one was interested. The silence was frightening. No one talked. Only a few people from Tzeiz were in line for the shower. My chances of getting in today increased.

Around midday the Magdeburg group got in line. A day and a half had gone by and there had been no roll call, and if there was no roll call, there was no food. I was a little surprised that the line was not long. When we had gotten off the train we had been at least 200! Where were the others? Were they piled up in the snow?

It was finally my turn to shower. It was no different from the previous times. Luckily, this time the clothes I got back were almost completely dry. At least I would not have to sleep in damp clothes that night, as I had to do after the shower at Magdeburg.

The groups began to get organized. Night fell. We had not received anything to eat for two days. The lineup came to an end. I was not interested in the size of the other groups, but I was shocked at the size of the Magdeburg group. When we were counted, we were only forty people!

I should have been happy that I had survived and was still functioning. The few people from Magdeburg that talked to each other said that we should stay together. After all, we knew each other. No one mentioned that we had dwindled in size to forty people. I saw no one my age in the group. I was the only one left from the youth group that had worked the night shift at Magdeburg. Several people in our small group were almost like the *muselmänner* at Magdeburg. Now I could clearly see that there was no rhyme or reason to who would survive. It was not necessarily the young or the strong who remained alive. The one-week journey from Magdeburg to Buchenwald and the two-day wait in quarantine for the showers had brought the final number down to only forty.

We left the quarantine. I roused myself in anticipation of the change, especially looking forward to food distribution at the permanent place. We arrived at a huge camp not far from the showers. I immediately observed that there were no prisoners here, and that the structure did not resemble the regular buildings for prisoners. The entire structure was made of bricks, with no doors or windows. It looked as if construction had been suspended. The *kapo* in charge told us that because it was already dark we could not be housed in the regular barracks. Therefore, we were to sleep here tonight and tomorrow we would go to our permanent barracks.

Bread distribution went quickly. We entered the barrack in an orderly manner and each person found a place to lie down. We passed the night on the floor of the big rooms. After I lay down by the wall a draft of wind froze my bones. I tried finding a better place, and I was not alone. Throughout the night there were people coming and going from room to room through the central hall, but it made no difference. It was not only cold throughout the building, it was also completely dark. Only the snow lit up the openings. Most of us could not fall asleep. I tried to recall the camp as I remembered it. I could faintly recall how it looked a few months ago. I looked forward to the next day. I strongly hoped that I would not be sent back to the infamous Block 56. I still remembered the behavior of the Ukrainians who ruled there.

Dawn broke. We waited impatiently to be brought to our permanent barracks. I did not have a clue where most of the people were taken. I was placed in a group that was ushered between the camp fences to an area the *kapo* called the *"Invalides lager"* (Invalids camp). It was only many days later that I learned that the Block I was assigned, Block 66, was called the *"Kinder Block"* (the children's block).

When I arrived the *kapo* asked for my country of origin. I was surprised. This was the first time since I had arrived at the camps that I was asked about my origins. The explanation I received was that Block 66 was divided into two wings: those from Hungary on the left, and those from Poland on the right. I could not understand the significance of the separation; we were all Jews here.

The bunks in both wings were similar to those I had known from all the other camps. One obvious difference was the iron furnace in the entrance between the two wings which I encountered for the first time. I did not understand the usefulness of having a stove between the two wings. I got an empty bunk on the top row.

I slowly acclimated to the place. For me life here was like the Garden of Eden compared to Magdeburg. We did not go to work at all, since we belonged to the Invalids camp located at the far end of Buchenwald. I wandered around outdoors with nothing to do, trying to get to know the place. I did not discover anything new. The bath house and latrines were built exactly like the previous camps I had inhabited. Within a few days I realized that the name "*Invalids Camp*" was justified. Dozens of *muselmänner* wandered around the yard in a slow, frightening manner. There had been *muselmänner* at Magdeburg as well, but since I was away at work every day except for the rest days, I only saw a few of them. Here, it was a common sight. Even on very cold days I would see them huddled against the walls of the barracks.

Toasted Bread and Tefillin[25]

There was order in Block 66. Two French communists were responsible for the two wings. For days on end we did not

---

[25]   *Tefillin* (also called phylacteries) - a set of small black leather boxes containing scrolls of parchment inscribed with verses from the Torah. They are attached to the body with leather straps and worn by Orthodox Jewish men on their head and arm during weekday morning prayers.

hear from them. Only when arguments broke out between the prisoners would they appear and try to restore order. I found it hard to get used to the harsh squabbling between the Polish and the Hungarian Jews. I did not know the cause. As I saw it, the main problem was lack of a common language: the Poles spoke Yiddish at home, but most of the Hungarians did not. Over time I became friendly with people from both sides.

The weather grew less cold as winter came to an end. I would go outdoors and walk around the Block, trying to get acquainted with the inhabitants. I got friendly with a Polish boy and tried to get him to talk. He did not talk about home. A Hungarian boy asked me afterwards how I could be friendly with someone from the other wing. "You just have to talk", I answered. The boy looked at me as if I had discovered something new.

The Polish boy explained the reason for the chasm separating the Poles and Hungarians. It had begun at Auschwitz. All those sent by transport to Auschwitz and had managed to survive Dr. Mengele's selection went through the "processing routine" that included removing their civilian clothes, shaving, showers and the clothing warehouse. In each hall permanent *kapos* were responsible for the process. The *kapos* chose helpers from each new transport. When Jews arrived from Poland the *kapos* would choose from among them. Later, when the transports from Hungary arrived, they took additional helpers. Some workers were not replaced frequently because a certain level of skill was needed, for example the crematorium workers who burned the corpses of those murdered, or those who collected and sorted the Jews' belongings known as the "Canada group" because Canada was thought to be a country with great riches. I remembered that going through the showers at Birkenau I was pushed and shoved through by Polish men. When I was at Magdeburg, they took a boy from my group and appointed him a vice-*kapo*. He immediately became violent and aggressive, and carried out the *kapo's* orders diligently. I was afraid to approach him as an acquaintance; his job set him above us. Additional food and clothing turn a prisoner into a different creature. I always remembered him with deep hatred but I did not connect this to his country of origin. And now I did not participate in the separation of the Hungarians and Poles in Block 66 at Buchenwald. I only sought companionship.

Since we did not go to work I spent the days walking around the yard, to the inside fence and back to the barrack. It was not far, and I could do this several times in a day. Little by little I recovered from the strain of the difficult trip from Magdeburg. I could not shake off the memory of the quarantine, and I still wondered how the Magdeburg group had been decimated. At least those who had gotten as far as the quarantine could have remained alive, had it not been for the German desire for "strict order".

There was very little food in Block 66 since no one here worked. Most of the people in the Invalids camp were, like me, prisoners who had been brought back from Buchenwald sub-camps. We arrived in a state of exhaustion. I had no other explanation for the many *muselmänner* lying around the camp grounds. There was no snow but it was unbearably cold. I was still without underpants, but there was no opportunity to get to the clothes warehouse. Actually, I did not even know if there was a clothes warehouse here.

After a few days I met an older man who claimed he knew me. It turned out that he had been with my father and me at Sárvár, and that we had arrived together at Auschwitz. I did not recognize him at first. I found it hard to believe that the person standing in front of me was the same joker who would entertain the SS at Sárvár with his sleight of hand card tricks. I remembered him as a smiling, happy young man. I asked him if he knew the fate of my father. He told me that he clearly remembered that my father had begun to limp as a result of a blow he had received at work, and that after he was wounded the SS men harassed him because of his inability to work. He thought that my father had died from a beating he got from the SS. I did not know what to make of his story. At first I began thinking about my home and family, but my present life led me to stop dwelling on these matters.

The sight of so many *muselmänner* on the grounds was not encouraging. We were completely indifferent toward them, but sometimes I thought that if I got too close I could catch something from them. I got used to the Invalids camp. Sometimes I visited the public latrine and watched the "business" conducted there. We had absolutely no possessions. It was there that I also picked up "reliable" news that the allies were advancing and the German forces were being routed. Our return from Magdeburg to Buchenwald was explained thus: "the Russians were approaching Berlin, which was near Magdeburg. The Germans had returned us from there so we would not be liberated." In the latrine I also heard that none of us would get out alive, so that no one would find out about the camps. The Germans planned to destroy Buchenwald as the final revenge.

The stories did not bother me. All I wanted was to make it through one day at a time. Sometimes I worried that I would not wake up in the morning, like many others. I did not want to die. I still had dreams about the outside world! Sometimes I would stand near the fence, looking out, and ask myself what life was like out there.

One day I thought that instead of walking around outside I should go back to the bunk and sleep during the day. If I slept, perhaps I would manage to dream about a different life. I had never dreamt in my sleep. My dreams always came as I was waking up, and I had total control over them. If I wanted to I could eat luscious meals, and if I got tired of feasting I could move on to another topic. For example, what would I do if I got out of Buchenwald alive? Here I encountered a problem with my beloved mother. She had always harbored a strong desire that I would be an observant Torah student. How could

I tell her that this was impossible? Nothing was left to believe in! What remained was only Block 66 of the Invalids camp, the bare ground and the barbed wire.

I returned to the block, climbed up to the bunk and prepared to fall asleep. I was tired of walking around. On the bunk beside me was an unfamiliar new person. We began to talk. I told him about my recent experiences, and he told me new stories about a different life he had experienced. He was a few years older than me. He talked like a "know-it-all", and I was never bored in his company. His name was Utzi, a typical Hungarian name. I learned his full name, Ehud Walter, only when we were liberated. The whole block soon knew his story. Utzi was born in Palestine. During the Arab revolt of 1936-1939 his family decided to return to Transylvania. Part of the family remained in Eretz Israel, but all those who returned were exterminated in Auschwitz.

I was amazed to see someone who was born in Palestine, the Jewish homeland. At home we had not talked much about that country. My mother believed that only when the Messiah came would we all reach the Land of Israel, after the dead were resurrected of course. I became friends with Utzi, as I had with others before.

Block 66 was awfully crowded and it was hard to sleep at night. If I tried to talk to Utzi at night, there would immediately be a commotion from below:

"Quiet! We want to sleep!" As if what we lacked was sleep. Were it not for our empty stomachs we could sleep during the day as well.

Utzi was a very calm person, and this would drive me crazy. He had an opinion on every subject in the world, and there was no arguing with him. We also had quiet days of course. I was surprised to discover an unusual habit of his: sometimes he would keep a small piece of his bread, which was doughy and heavy, and knead that small piece for hours until it was a grayish lump - then he would mold it into a chess piece. He kept the finished pieces in a small bag, guarding them against anyone who tried to eat them.

In Block 66 there was a French prisoner responsible for discipline and for our medical needs. We assumed he was a doctor. Utzi had an infected wound on his buttocks. Every other day the Frenchman would lay Utzi on a table and try to clean the wound. There was no disinfectant here of course, and injuries were treated exactly as in Magdeburg: wiped with tissue paper dipped in water. The Frenchman never forgot to announce to the entire wing: "come see how I treat the holy *"tuches"* (backside) from Palestine!", and Utzi would beam with pleasure when his birthplace was mentioned. The Frenchman also treated my infected ankle with the same roll of tissue paper. He had nothing to offer me except a pat on the back. During one of the treatments I told the Frenchman about the orderly at Magdeburg; how he would amputate infected fingers and be done with the problem brought to him. It was probably the daily routine horrors in the midst of which we lived that prompted his reaction: he asked me if it would be worthwhile to amputate Utzi's backside and be done with the infection.

Skirmishes broke out very often in Block 66. There was no need to look for a pretext as the opportunities were limitless. After lineup for example, everyone pushed to get inside. Since there was only one entrance for both wings, brawls and arguments would erupt. I never got involved in them. The sight of the feeble prisoners raising their arms in an attempt to hit each other, walking skeletons clustered together and pushing each other around to no advantage was ridiculous. Another source of endless arguments was the furnace between the two wings. Sometimes a few boards were found to heat the furnace. It was hard to crowd close to get warm. Only the strong ones succeeded. Someone had an idea to warm the bread on the sides of the blazing furnace, and immediately there was a long line of prisoners who wanted to toast their bread. Then the pushing and shoving would start and the Polish-Hungarian war would reach a climax. Once in a while I also wanted to enjoy toasted bread. I would stand in line and wait, eating some bread as I waited. I usually finished the bread before it was my turn.

Time and time again reasons for quarrels arose. Someone would remember that his friend had been kicked in Auschwitz by Polish Jews, or Hungarian Jews, and he would rush to get even... One day we heard that the Hungarian prisoners were hiding a bag with *tefillin*, and several prisoners would wait in line to pray. Most of us were indifferent to their prayers, but not a red-headed prisoner from the Polish wing. He simply decided that there was no God and no need for *tefillin*, went up to the person who was praying and tore them off! No one got excited or tried to separate the protagonists. When asked why he had started the squabble the perpetrator answered that he had given up on the Creator of the Universe a long time ago.

I began keeping to myself. I was no longer interested in conversations with people. I felt that we had exhausted every topic. I was tired of listening to imaginary menus, and the different interpretations of the strength of the allied forces approaching Buchenwald only increased my depression. Some people exaggerated to the point of talking about food packages dropped over Buchenwald. It was unnecessary to point out that no one ever saw any such packages.

We learned that among the veteran prisoners at Buchenwald there were many who had worked at a metal plant in the area which, rumor had it, manufactured weapons. These prisoners were mostly well-organized communists. There was talk in the latrines that as the Germans were being defeated these veteran prisoners would defend the other prisoners against the SS threat of annihilating the entire camp population. They would do this with weapons they had managed to obtain for themselves. I asked myself if their rescue plans included the Jews. I remembered well the first time I was in Buchenwald. I had felt no support from the veteran prisoners or the Ukrainians, to the contrary, only hatred. Every nation has enemies, but hatred of Jews unites them all! At any rate, rumors at Buchenwald about communists and veterans rescuing Jews were the ones I believed least of all.

Rumors

Sometimes new prisoners stood out on the grounds. One of them was David, a tall thin youth who ran around the camp all day long. He spoke Hungarian, but it was hard to understand him because he stammered. He looked like a scarecrow because of his special clothes. We all wore the same striped clothes, but not David, he was so tall. I will describe him from the feet up: Dutch wooden shoes, two bare limbs, above them light green riding breeches, and above them a bright red Hussar jacket with brass buttons that had at one time sparkled. There was no telling where he got his scarecrow outfit. He stood out so vividly that the Ukrainians tore off most of his brass buttons when he was in the latrine.

David kept us awake with his long nightly monologues. Although he slept on the bottom bunk his voice could be heard throughout the Hungarian wing of the Block. He talked continuously about food, choosing the ingredients to match his taste. He never mentioned weekday dishes, only Shabbat and holiday delicacies starred in his monologues. His Friday night meals always began with two thick slices of *challah*", heavily coated with poppy seeds; the fish course also included two identical slices of *challah*. Next of course came meat soup with *kreplach* (filled dumplings), and for dessert once again two thick slices of *challah* coated with poppy seeds. None of us argued with him about his selection for the feast. Were it not for his stuttering we could have been asleep well before midnight.

At the same time we noticed that our portions at the invalids camp were shrinking. This explained the increasing number of *muselmänner* in Block 66. Many of them did not get out of their bunks all day long, just lay there staring into space. We did not converse with them, as if they had a contagious disease. I would stand and watch the other *muselmänner* who would sit, leaning against the wall of the Block, not moving as if frozen in time. No one knew exactly how a person turned into a *muselmänn*. Everyone got the same portion of bread and here in the invalids camp no one went to work. I sat down next to a *muselmänn* and stared at him. Perhaps the answer was to be found deep in a man's soul? Perhaps it was the desperation and lack of hope for a changed life? I tried talking to him. Unintelligible mumbling came out of his mouth. I did not understand a word. He moved his head, he had heard me! I said to him: "You are holding a bread portion in your hand, why not eat it?" The *muselmänn* moved his arm like a figure in a puppet theater and began eating slowly. He scattered crumbs all around and it looked as if he was having difficulty swallowing. The bread stayed in his open mouth. I could see the inside his mouth and his stained teeth. It reminded me of the corpses I had seen in Magdeburg when I carried out the orders of Laci the overseer, pulling out gold teeth from the mouths of the dead – and I shuddered. Maybe they were truly contagious? Why in the world had I sat down next to him? No one talks to them and most of them lay separated from the other prisoners! The situation I had created for myself left me feeling terrorized for the remainder of the day. I refrained from looking at *muselmänner* for several days.

The inactivity and preoccupation with food frustrated me greatly. The one-sided conversation with the *muselmänn* gave me no peace. I wanted to prove to myself that I was healthy and strong, even though wandering around the camp left me very tired. By that time I knew many people in the Hungarian wing. I would look them over and try to determine if our physical condition was still reasonable. I did not see myself. I would sometimes touch my hip and could feel that it was all bone! When I lay down I did not feel anything, but sitting hurt me and wore me out. My ribs had been sticking out for a while. Sometimes I would count them, reminded of the science lessons in school, or to be precise of the skeleton in the science room. The Invalids camp was populated by walking skeletons. In my imagination I could see all of us taking off our striped clothes only to become models in the science room…

But in Buchenwald even bones were not left alone. Everything was consumed. Someone told me that after the bodies were burned, only small bones remained in the oven after the ashes were swept out. What thoughts were these? Did some kind of madness grab hold of me? Not likely, when I talked to friends I talked normally. It was my wild imagination that gave me no peace!

As I entered the block the Frenchman was talking. Everyone had crowded around to listen. Perhaps he had some news? The Frenchman explained that the war would soon be over. "If we remain alive, we (the Christians) will see to it that the Jews are temporarily imprisoned, until we settle accounts with the Nazis! You Jews, with your Bible, are full of compassion, and would probably forgive and forget too soon!"

I asked if he included the Ukrainians among the Christians who would seek revenge, especially the Ukrainians in Block 56. He gave me a startled look: "How come you know Block 56?"

I told him that I was once a resident of that block, and how much the Ukrainians had "loved" us. I went up a notch in the Frenchman's eyes. He asked me what I had done there, but I told him that I did not remember anything from those days.

Actually, the Frenchman talked a lot and I had no patience to listen to him. Now he was explaining to everyone that if food was sent to Buchenwald we would have to be careful not to eat everything that came our way: "Eat carefully because the stomachs are shrunk and the bowels are too narrow to hold a lot of food!" The Frenchman talked, and I recalled how I would search my pockets to find a forgotten crumb.

This was at the beginning of March 1945. A month earlier I had turned seventeen. I did not notice the spring arriving. I was worried about my physical weakness. I became aware of how much weaker I had become, when instead of climbing onto the bunk during the day to rest I preferred sitting against the wall of the block outside. There was a simple reason for this: it was now hard for me to climb up to the third tier of bunks. Sometimes someone would give me a push to lift me up, and I would feel helpless and embarrassed. At night I had a hard time sleeping. I was afraid of the dismal sight that would await me in the morning in Block 66 - of another prisoner who continued to sleep, his life ended without a whimper. A still silence accompanied his end, without a friend, without someone who knew him. The *muselmänn* could not even be identified.

My thoughts alone were wearing me out. Someone once told me that if I wanted to stop a troublesome thought I should bang my fist against a hard wall. The physical pain would distract me from dwelling on my troubles. I tried it several times, without much success.

In the sunlight of early spring we sat slumped along the walls of the barracks, soaking up the weak sunshine. And then I recalled the speech an SS man would give each time I entered another camp: "Never look a German talking to you in the face. Remove your hat, and be as silent as reptiles and as low as grass on the ground!" And now this exact thing had come about! I was sitting on the frozen ground of Buchenwald, silent as a reptile and as low as grass. Only deep inside me I was still alive and hoping…to live another day.

We stopped talking about food. There was virtually no food in Block 66 at the Buchenwald concentration camp. From time to time there were small trips to the assembly grounds. All were counted once again, surely bread would be distributed. I peered around, and had the doubtful pleasure of seeing my friends the *muselmänner*: skin and bones and perhaps a bit of soul left inside...

I wondered what the others thought about me. Was I also a *muselmänn*? Perhaps I was. Once again I felt my ribs. I could easily count them. I felt chilly, so I drew my head between my shoulders. What luck that I had lined my hat with a piece of blanket I had fit inside. Everyone said that you had to keep your head warm. My feet were really freezing. I could not tuck them under me; I did not have the strength to sit on them like I used to. It didn't matter!

Soon it would be night and I would have to move from the wall and return to the bunk. The last time I was at Buchenwald I could climb up to the third tier, almost like a cat. Today I will try to do it by myself. If I succeed my friends will undoubtedly say "one more *muselmänn*". No! I am not a *muselmänn* yet! I am alive! I can feel! My eyes still see everything, my mouth still talks with my neighbor by the wall... but he does not answer. His eyes stare into space.

I succeeded. I climbed up to the bunk all on my own. Tomorrow I will also try to do it by myself. Tomorrow the sun will also shine!

The entire area of the invalids camp was separated from the other areas by a fence. I did not know those living on the other side of this fence. Someone in the Hungarian wing told me that at the edge of the camp, where it reached the electric fence, there were barracks surrounded by a built wall, instead of a barbed wire fence. He told me excitedly that he had managed to get a look into the partitioned area (apparently I was not the only wanderer in the camp) and discovered that there were well-run barracks in that section. He reported that he saw women in the yard! He thought they were "field whores", prisoners who serviced the SS, usually under coercion.

The story aroused my curiosity, but I did not join his walks. I was not among the brave who wandered outside the invalids camp. I stayed close to Block 66, afraid that I might miss something while I was away.

Evacuation Means Death

March was drawing to a close. The size of the food portions for those in the invalids camp shrank once again, and the effect was first be seen on the older prisoners. The exemplary order that had been a hallmark of the camp was not what it used to be. Every day new prisoners joined Block 66. Life here was considered safer than in other areas of the camp, since this was the *Kinder Block*! Even now there were adults who believed that the *Kinder Block* would not be harmed. It was very overcrowded. Rumors were flying, and like many in camp I also thought the Germans intended to liquidate Buchenwald.

Sounds of allied bombings were heard frequently in the camp area. It was hard to determine their distance and direction, but the sound signaled a definite change in the course of the war. Perhaps we would actually be liberated? I did not even dare dream about it. Rumors about the camp's liquidation persisted!

The next day at morning lineup we were surprised by a large group of SS men who arrived at the invalids camp. They were accompanied by dozens of prisoners we did not recognize, with white ribbons on their sleeves. They surrounded the grounds and pushed us in the direction of the main assembly grounds. Chaos and confusion ensued. Apparently the guards were not well-trained in their new job.

The march began, but most of the people scattered along the way and many of us returned to the invalids camp. During the commotion the sirens sounded and most of the guards ran for cover. The explosions were heard throughout the camp, but it was hard to tell where they fell. At any rate, the evacuation planned for this day did not take place.

I understood that the time had come: rumors about the camp evacuation were materializing. Clearly evacuation meant eradication. We were nearing the end of the war and fate was once again playing tricks on us.

Towards evening there was a loss of electricity and we were able to return to the Block. The Frenchman tried to calm things down. Rumors spread that the communist leadership in the main camp had revolted and prevented the evacuation. I had a hard time falling asleep. Bread was not distributed that day.

The next day was quiet. Surprisingly information reached us from the communists in the upper camp. One of them came to Block 66 with new identification tags for us. The communists ordered the Jewish prisoners to remove the yellow stripe next to the number on their clothes and replace it with the new tags. This was done to sabotage SS plans to remove the Jewish prisoners from the camp. Their concern for us was encouraging. Suddenly we forgot about our gnawing hunger. One more day without food was not the end of the world!

The next day another lineup was attempted. The order to line up was issued and this time we were promised that we would get food. We had been conditioned to the fact that we never received food until we were counted, but many in the Block did not believe the promises and did not want to go outside. The SS men tried to lure them out by "tempting" them with bread.

I was among those who went. We stood quietly in the evening lineup, hoping against hope that bread would be delivered after the count. At least the threatened evacuation had not taken place that day. Suddenly everything was so quiet, even squabbles were not heard. We were very confused.

Counts were held twice a day but still no bread was distributed. Nine hundred children were standing in groups according to barrack and nationality. Two hours of counting, and the numbers did not match. As long as the numbers did not match, there was no bread. Here and there someone would collapse from weakness. The prisoner was dragged to the side, and the count would start again. Most of those who collapsed were *muselmänner*. I prayed in my heart that I would not reach that stage. I already had several symptoms: my knees and stomach were swollen, but I came to every lineup. I had to survive!

The lineup ended and we returned to our barracks. I could hardly climb up to my bunk on the top row. Sometimes friends down below would help and push me up. It was so difficult for me but I finally made it. I wanted to end up facing the front, but instead my head was by the barrack wall. When I was overcome by hunger I would smell the tar rubbed into the wood, trying to imagine that it smelled of some unknown food.

I do not know if I fell asleep or was half unconscious. Someone from below was shaking my leg…I woke up…shouts! Line up for counting! Was it already morning? Had a new day begun? No, it was the lineup before sleep. There would not be bread until tomorrow!

And again a day went by…

Block 66 sleeps.

Everything is barren and desolate…

The black barracks, the glittering symmetrical paths…

Complete desolation, no sound!

No cat, no dog, no bird chirping.

The night is black; the whole world is black.

The guard towers stand erect,

The searchlight turns…

We are alone here with the guards.

The world is sleeping.
Morning…
Night has passed –
And I am alive!

In the morning a commotion broke out in the Block,
and no one tried to calm us down. The Frenchman, who was
actually in charge of the Block, had no words of advice. By
now we already knew that anyone caught on the assembly
grounds was directly removed from Buchenwald. We did
not know for sure what had been the fate of those prisoners
taken to the other side of the camp gates, but the possibilities
were terrifying.

There had been no water in the camp for two days.
Rumor had it that the *Hitler Jugend* [26] (Hitler Youth) were the
culprits. Supposedly they had blown up the pumps in the city
of Weimar which supplied the camp's drinking water. Knowing
this we got the idea to hide in the sewage pipes at Buchenwald.
The water works were in back of the invalids camp. Hordes of
us ran in that direction.

The scene there was sickening. No water ran in the pipes.
We got into the pipes that were so wide we could easily move
around in them. No, we could not stay there, the pipes were
full of garbage. Several people began picking through the
garbage, finding beet peelings, apparently from the central
kitchen. They were rotten and I did not touch them. But some
people wiped them off as best they could and ate them. We
were ravenous. I could not remember how long it had been
since we had last eaten.

We returned to the Block after a few hours, passing the
night on our bunks. It was impossible to fall asleep, fear of
evacuation was palpable. Every sound from outside the
Block was a source of panic and dread for me. I curled up,

---

[26] *Hitler Jugend* – The Hitler Youth, the youth organization of the Nazi Party in
Germany.

and with great effort tried not to think of my empty stomach, even though it was very irritating. I asked my neighbor in the bunk how long one could live without food. There was no answer. The muselmänner in the bunk were silent and no one exchanged a word with them. When we ran to hide in the sewage pipes we left them sitting in the yard leaning against the side of the Block. They were also absent from the lineups.

Apparently I had dozed off again. Morning finally came. What awaited us today? In the Hungarian wing someone suggested that as soon as the SS men came with the evacuation team we should try to climb into the attic. Several people tried to pry open the wooden planks in the roof and happily announced that there was room there.

The lineup began again in the morning. It was impossible to avoid. We went out and stood restlessly during the count. Again they announced, "Be quiet, and as soon as the count is over, the bread will get here!" And again we were misled. Instead of the promised bread, the evacuation team arrived at the lineup!

I was led with some others in the direction of the gate, praying that there would be an air raid alarm. Only an alarm could save us. On one opportunity that the path curved I managed to sneak away and run back to the Block. Here a surprise awaited me. Some people had succeeded in getting into the attic! The creaking boards could easily be heard. SS men were seen heading towards our Block. We stood dumbfounded, crowding against each other. The SS men were suspicious and hit the ceiling with their rifle butts. It came crashing down, to the sound of the Germans' laughter. The commotion was terrible. I tried to get outside. The SS men beat us indiscriminately with their rifle butts, but I escaped their blows. However my friend Utzi was hit hard with a rifle butt; he tried protecting his private parts and the blow hit his fingers.

The SS men left the Block. I did not know what they were

plotting. It was getting dark and we knew that we had made it through one more day.

Another night in the invalid camp… hunger was gnawing at our innards, but no one complained. We were sure that the SS men were not going to leave us alone. The front had to be far away if the Germans had time to "take care" of the Jews. The Frenchman encouraged us, telling us that liberation was near. We had to get by for just a few more days! I was very scared during those days, but I did not dare tell my friends. Only the will to survive gave me strength.

The next day, surprisingly, there was no lineup. I wandered around the grounds trying not to think about food. I observed the dozens of *muselmänner* lying around, and I asked myself if they would live, even if the war ended. I would touch them with unexplained curiosity. None of them responded. Only their eyes bulged out of their sockets. Their heads looked as if they had shrunk; their striped hats falling to their protruding ears, and their sunken cheeks highlighting their jaw bones. I waited for one of them to say a word…then I would immediately get up with difficulty and hurry back to the Block. Perhaps something had happened while I was away?

The next day the lineup was held as usual, but the alarm began before it ended. We were happy for one more day in Block 66. Suddenly I felt close to my Block. It felt good to climb up to the bunk, even though I needed help from my friends to make it up there. During the day rumors flew that Gustav, who was responsible for the Polish wing, had chosen a group of children from Block 66 and had taken them to a hiding place in the camp to prevent their evacuation. The entire group had been caught near the central assembly grounds and taken out of the camp. Only Gustav was released. I did not know Gustav, but when I saw him from a distance I was always impressed by his dress: he went around in a Polish army uniform and wore shiny boots.

We were all concerned about our situation. Our lives

hung by a thread. Would the SS men come to evacuate us, or not? Days went by. According to my calculations we had not received food for eight days. By now I was very feeble and came down from the bunk just to go to the latrine: a need which became less frequent as the days went by.

One day the Frenchman burst into the Block, announcing excitedly that the occupying armies were approaching Buchenwald! There was a danger, he said, that the SS men would break into the camp with weapons and eliminate everyone. According to the Frenchman, the Germans wanted to destroy any and all evidence of their atrocities, but it could also simply be revenge. He organized boards and mattresses, whatever he could find in order to seal the windows, explaining that: "the Germans could shoot rounds of machine-gun fire into the Block! Remember, this is a significant day!" Perhaps we would remain alive despite everything!

We were confused and happy: everything would soon come to an end. Sounds of gunfire were heard from all directions of the camp.

Suddenly there was complete silence. We opened the doors, our curiosity got the better of us. In other parts of the camp people were already running around, and cries of joy could be heard: "They came down from the watchtowers! They are fleeing into the forest!"

I did not know what to do or what to think. Could it be that the day had arrived? We heard the noise of tanks approaching the fences. We were so surprised that we did not dare go far from the Block. I waited by the barracks, totally exhausted. I felt that my legs would not carry me for another two steps. I sat on the ground and leaned against the wall… how was it possible to absorb this news? We were confused. Everyone talked at once; no one understood what was being said. I wanted to shout so badly, but I was struck dumb; my voice stuck in my dry throat and I could only shout inwardly:

Here I am alive! I had survived in spite of everything! Against all odds I had survived!

7.

Liberation – I am a Youth Again

In the afternoon, announcements were heard over loudspeakers throughout the camp. Our ears took in every word. The voice was talking to us! We are no longer prisoners; we are human beings. What are they saying? They are looking for volunteers for the kitchen to peel potatoes! No, it's not a mistake, but why bother peeling the potatoes?

I count the minutes. The food will arrive soon! Revolutionary. Inside the Block they still refuse to believe the new reality. The glad tidings are still hard to digest. Nonetheless the joy is complete as the Poles and the Hungarians embrace each other - the wolf shall dwell with the lamb. The Germans do not reappear with reinforcements.

Over the past months I had not believed that the Germans would ever be defeated. But here, the impossible had happened! Potatoes were being cooked for us! In my mind's eye I saw the steam rising as the potatoes were being peeled…I would soon take a bite… How many times had I dreamt of boiled potatoes melting in my mouth!

A commotion is heard from the direction of the assembly grounds. The giant containers had arrived, the lid was lifted, the steam was rising…the line is orderly. We all untie our bowls from our bodies, breathless with anticipation. It is my turn. I receive nearly a full bowl of unpeeled potatoes…hot, very hot! Ceremoniously I peel, eat, peel, eat. I leave the peelings nearby. My stomach is full, a little swollen. The bowl is emptied quickly.… Now I just want to sleep. I climb up to the bunk but cannot fall asleep. When will daylight come, so I can try to grasp the meaning of Liberation Day? I fell asleep.

The ruckus begins in the block with the first light of day. Noise, discussions, arguments…everyone standing in groups, all talking at once. I move around the Block as if intoxicated. Every minute I join another group to hear the stories. It is beyond imagination. Some people wander around the camp to witness the wide open gates with their own eyes!

A huge container of sweetened coffee arrives. There is much shoving , but no fights break out. Everyone tries to guess what will happen. I overheard "our" Frenchman talking with a *kapo* from another Block: "Look at the joy of the youth! Imagine that within a few days, they will not just eat a lot of food, but food that tastes good!" Could that really be, I wondered.

My friends were planning to go for a walk around the camp, to taste the freedom, to smell it. I decided to join them. I was very tired. I suddenly felt that it was hard for me to walk. My stomach was swollen and my knees had swelled grotesquely. I remembered how just two days ago I had wondered whether I looked like a *muselmänn*. They also had protruding knees and toothpick legs. At the central assembly grounds I left the group. I decided to visit Block 56; the block where I my stay at Buchenwald had begun. Of course I did not know anyone. No one even glanced at me. Suddenly everyone was confused and busy with no time to look around. I reached the kitchen area. The yard was full of large empty vats, and there was great commotion in the kitchen. I did not get too close. I could not shake off the feeling that the kitchen was "off limits" for me.

I sat down to rest. I could not take in everything that was happening around me. All at once a loaded truck appeared and dozens of people volunteered to help unload it. I could hear Ukrainian being spoken. They were everywhere, and they all looked as strong as hooligans. Dozens of slaughtered pigs were taken off the truck and carted to the kitchen. My joy was complete: there would be plenty of food for us in the coming days!

One pig remained on the cart and the Ukrainians pushed it into a corner of the grounds. Within minutes the attack began. I do not know where all the people with knives came from. Each person cut himself a piece of meat and ran away. I was impressed by their speed. Within minutes only the pig's head and feet were left in the cart.

I went back to Block 66 to make sure I had not missed anything. There were no clear instructions about what we should do, but we all returned to our barracks. I could not imagine any fundamental change, except for food, that would come regularly.

The next meal was filling. Suddenly we could not finish a full bowl of thick soup, since we were accustomed to the watery liquid since our first days in the camps. The soup was so thick that it was easy to identify the cubes of potatoes and strips of lard floating in the bowl. The Frenchman assembled us in the barrack and warned us not to take second helpings and not to eat too much, because it could harm our stomach. I did not particularly believe him, even though I could feel the pressure in my stomach. Food affected each of us differently. I felt that my bowels were blocked. I recalled that I had not visited the latrine for two days. On the other hand a Hungarian boy from my bunk complained that he had severe diarrhea, sat all day in the latrine, and did not know what to do. I told him that the liberators would soon set up a clinic and he could get help there.

I was filthy from head to toe. Water had not yet reached the invalids camp which was at the far end of Buchenwald. We had to walk to the center of the camp for drinking water. No one talked about a real bath yet. I found some clean striped clothes in one of the Blocks. I changed clothes quickly, and no one bothered to look at me or stop me. I felt a lot better, but walking was still very difficult.

We talked and talked without end, but no one mentioned home. We spoke in general terms about leaving Buchenwald. We simply did not know what was going on outside camp, and we were still in total shock.

A group of American soldiers appeared at Block 66. They looked to us like giants! They inspected the place, accompanied by camp functionaries whom I did not know. The *muselmänner* were still lying along the walls of Block 66, soaking up the sun's warmth. They lay wrapped in blankets. Only that evening did we learn that the liberators had issued an order not to change anything in the *Invalids* camp. That meant even leaving the *muselmänner* on the grounds so that as many visitors as possible could photograph the atrocities at the camp.

I climbed up to the bunk, worn out. Before falling asleep, I recalled that while changing clothes, I had forgotten to take the potato peels. Someone would no doubt find them…

The next day I went with several boys to the crematorium. I had heard that the place was brimming with American soldiers and journalists, and I really wanted to see them. No one stopped us. The first time I had been in Buchenwald, when I belonged to Block 56, the Ukrainians would collect the corpses from the blocks and cart them to the crematorium. I still remember the Ukrainian who said to me: "Jew boy, soon we'll be taking you there!" And here I was, going to visit the grounds of the crematorium.

The place was much smaller than I had imagined. Lots of people were milling around the entrance grounds. Several days had passed since the liberation, and they were still taking pictures of the corpses waiting to be burned! I mingled among them. One of the veterans of the upper camp served as a guide, explaining to the journalists the camp routines: "the wagon arrives here, at this end of the building…there is a kind of square window under the building, with a wide tin-plated chimney coming out of it. This was how they slid the bodies into the hall below, where they were undressed and the gold teeth pulled from their mouths... Nearby was a lift that brought the bodies to the crematorium... Do you see the stretcher on wheels near the door? The corpse was put there and sent into the crematorium. Poles with rakes were on hand to clean off the ashes and pull it back out...".

Everything was perfect, so well organized and orderly! There were no questions; everything was clear. We, the former prisoners, were also interested in all the details. I felt as if a demon was pushing me nearer, to see the remaining ashes after the fire. I already knew from previous stories at Auschwitz that all that was left after burning were small bones not completely consumed by the fire. I was not the only one who took a small bone out of the ash box as a memento. For a long time I kept it in an empty match box. Only when I reached Israel, at Magdiel School, was the bone taken by someone from the Tel Aviv Rabbinate[27] for burial.

I left the crematorium and trailed after the American soldiers, very impressed. They were all so pleasant and smiling! They could not get over the miracle they were witnessing here: boys so young who had remained alive. I would stand in front of a soldier and watch how he would search through his many pockets looking for something to pass out to the boys around him. There was no end to the wonder. The soldier would pull a surprise out of every pocket... It was the first time in my life I tasted chewing gum. I did not know you were supposed to spit it out after the flavor was gone, and swallowed it. One of the soldiers gave me a package of cigarettes. I lit a cigarette in amazement. Before I could inhale twice I felt dizzy and fell down, amidst the laughter of my friends. The tour wore me out. I felt overcome with weakness and returned to my good old bunk in Block 66.

---

[27] Rabbinate – the rabbinical authority of Judaism in Israel that has jurisdiction over many aspects of Jewish life in Israel, including Jewish burial.

Food was still our number one concern. We kept busy guessing what the next meal would be. Residents of the Block did not leave the camp area. We were still feeble and a bit frightened. Every day we heard of people who died from overeating.

Little by little we began to recuperate. The stronger ones began to venture outside the camp in the mornings. When they came back I asked them what they had done all day long and they told me countless stories. They had walked in the forests and had seen hundreds of bodies hanging from trees - Russian prisoners hung by the Germans during the last days before liberation. There were groups who chased suspicious looking Germans who tried to conceal their identity by wearing civilian clothes instead of their uniform. The pursuit took place around the camp. I loved hearing the heroic deeds of my friends. Soon I would be strong enough to go out with the others, to see what life was like outside the camp.

Several days later I was taken to an improvised American clinic. It was the first time I received real medical treatment for my infected heel. Treatment was courteous and caring. The medic washed my leg, rubbed it, and drained the pus from the wound in my heel. I saw the depth of the wound for the first time. He then put sulfa powder on it and bandaged it with cotton. I felt wonderful. They asked me if I wanted to stay in the infirmary for a few days, but I preferred to come back every day to have the bandage changed. I was amazed at the amount of equipment the American army had at its disposal.

Outside the camp a huge tent encampment was set up, and they had everything there! Kitchens, food storehouses and even hot showers in the tents ... everything aroused my curiosity. I walked around the entire encampment and the soldiers let me go anywhere I wanted in order to satisfy my curiosity. Everything was packed in cans, even cake. I was a bit overwhelmed by the amount of food they had. I did not dare eat too much. I believed the rumor that many had died from overeating.

It was announced in the Block that the following morning the Americans would begin compiling a list of names of those liberated at Buchenwald. I waited impatiently to be listed. This was an entirely novel experience. They asked me for my name, where I was born, my father's name, and also for the identification number I had received at Buchenwald. When I asked why they needed my number, I was told that they were preparing release papers from Buchenwald. After the registration process I was weighed. I had been eating quite a bit since the liberation, but even so, I weighed only 29 kilos!

The conquering army command was involved in every aspect of life at the camp. We learned that Buchenwald was the first camp to be liberated. The soldiers wandered everywhere, not missing any corner of the camp. They could not see enough. Shocked, they saw the physical condition of the *muselmänner,* especially the younger ones. Some of the American officers brought German citizens from Weimar to see the camp. They sent trucks to the city to bring them. That is how the Germans got to see Block 66. Most of the citizens were brought from their homes. There were doctors and pharmacists in white robes. Many of us joined the "guided tour" the American soldiers gave them.

While shown around they could only say one thing: "We never heard about or knew that a concentration camp existed. We knew there were work camps, but we did not know people were being starved and tortured there!"

Incredulously I heard what they said. In Magdeburg I had seen German citizens watching the punishment assemblies with pleasure every day. How could they stand in front of us calmly and brazenly nodding their heads? They were actual participants in our predicament! As far as I was concerned they did not need the tour to learn what they already knew.

Several days after liberation it was decided to move Block

66 outside the camp. The Americans housed us in the SS barracks, two-story buildings with bathrooms in the hallways. Luxury apartments! There was great rejoicing and excitement. The transfer was not complicated. We simply marched out of the camp... We now slept four or five to a room, on beds with mattresses. I do not know who came up with the idea, but the next day we were throwing the furniture we didn't need out the window. We started bonfires in the yard, and burned anything we could get our hands on. It was dangerous to pass under the windows.

While in the yard around the bonfire a boy from a nearby room complained terribly about severe diarrhea. I took him up to the building, sat him down by the wall and tried to convince him to go to the American clinic, but to no avail. He had apparently lost all desire to live. I pulled charred wood out of the bonfire, scraped off the charcoal, and tried to get him to take some of what was used in the camp to treat diarrhea. He died two days later. I found him in the same place where I had sat him down. No one could identify him and I did not know his name. He was taken away with the other corpses.

We gradually settled into our rooms. We came across some empty tin cans and arranged them on the shelves in our rooms. Each of us claimed a shelf where he kept leftover food in the cans, including cooked potato peels. We were unable to throw anything away. At midday the giant food vats would arrive amidst great clatter. We would line up by the rooms and fill our bowls with the thick soup. After we were full we would fish out the strips of pork fat that had been cooked with the vegetables. We could not finish eating it all, but could not bring ourselves to throw away food. So we kept the fat in the cans on the shelves, just in case we ever needed it.

One day I agreed to go with some friends to a *kumsitz*, a get-together around a campfire. We remembered how as children we would go into the forest and build campfires. Now we commandeered potatoes and bread, took the fat in the cans, and putting it all in a knapsack set out to build a fire. We did not get far because of the exhaustion that overcame us after walking only a few dozen meters.

I volunteered to cook. As a child I had spent a lot of time in my mother's kitchen. I suggested using the potatoes to make pancakes. Since we did not have a grater we crushed the potatoes with a stone, put the strips of fat in the food bowl - and the party began. The aroma arising from the fire was exhilarating. The pancakes were burned and had no salt: but it did not matter - this was our first celebration outside the camp.

Exploring the army base we found the SS supplies warehouse. Needless to say we were not the first ones there. We found the leather uniforms of the armored corps and we all grabbed jackets and trousers, even though they were too big for most of us in our condition. A few days later we learned that most of the leather outfits had been taken by the Ukrainian thugs. When the supplies warehouse was empty the Ukrainians came to our rooms and aggressively took the leather outfits we had taken for ourselves. The only items that remained in good supply were the special unit black SS caps. I wore the black SS cap with my striped camp clothes.

We found a huge storeroom full of meat cans. We filled our knapsacks and returned to our rooms where we filled the shelves. We opened a can, which had fatty pork, which I was afraid to eat because it had so much fat.

We came up with a new way of talking. We would ask each other, "What did you manage to commandeer?", and whoever had "commandeered" the most, gained the admiration of the others for his heroism and skill. I always seemed to arrive when it was too late. I was still too weak to run around to uncover all the possibilities. One day I found everyone gathered around the SS headquarters building. I went inside and found the rooms full of people searching through a huge file that filled several rooms. They were searching for documentation about the prisoners. I remembered the personal file that had been created for me the first day I arrived at Buchenwald – a photograph had been taken and personal information registered. The confusion was so great that only a few of us managed to find our files.

The building was huge and included many departments. I saw civilian clothes hanging on hangers in one room, on each lapel a name and an identification number. These dated back to the first years of the camp, when political prisoners who opposed the Nazis were sent there. Everything was organized. I went through the suit pockets and found personal papers. I saw small containers on the shelves in the room, marked with the identification numbers of the those who had been executed and containing their ashes.

In my explorations I came across a hall with a door that had been broken down. It was packed with bags closed with seals. Some of the seals were broken. The bags were filled with coins from various countries, including Hungary. It did not occur to me to touch them or take them. I knew beyond a doubt that I would never return to Hungary.

Cherries on the Train

The days went by and I had not yet begun to think of a plan for the future. I took no interest in what was happening outside of Buchenwald, as if the camp was my permanent home. All my plans were short-range: what I would do today, where I would go now. I made it a habit to visit the prisoners' quarters. Every few days I would go back to look at my Block. The place swarmed with journalists from everywhere as well as with American and British officers. I met an American soldier who spoke Yiddish. He had a million questions and as we spoke he could not stop crying. I knew that crying was all but natural and even necessary, but I could not understand why. There was no reason, the war was over!

And what about my family? I had already heard about my father; I knew he had been murdered in Auschwitz. I was sure that my mother and sister were not alive, no doubt that they had been taken to Auschwitz. What was left for me to cry about? Most of the time I asked for nothing but to survive, to show everyone that I had endured, to tell everyone about the Auschwitz, Magdeburg and Buchenwald monstrosities. Actually, who was I going to tell? I always imagined the entire world listening to me as I testified about the deeds of the SS, the devil that walked by our side, and the German population where not one righteous person had stood up. No need to cry. Crying arouses pity, and we don't need pity. I saw the citizens of Weimar when they toured the invalids camp. Not one of them shed a wretched tear. They just nodded their heads, said "Ah!", and returned to the city shocked by the filth and stench of the Jews. They no doubt hurried to take a shower so as not to contaminate their pure noble selves. And they were the people of culture! I continued to wander the winding paths of the camp. The American Jewish soldier remained there with his tears.

Finally I also joined a small group which decided to go into the city, into Weimar. Perhaps we would see how the Germans lived? Perhaps we would commandeer something special to eat? We left the camp and stood by the side of the road that led into town. Giant trucks filled with soldiers passed us by. One truck stopped, a soldier got off and asked us in broken German where we were headed. "Weimar!" we answered in unison. We were a group of five or six former prisoners. Two or three climbed up, and three, including me, remained standing, without the strength to climb up. The soldier smiled cheerfully and helped us into the truck.

The city was not far; the camp and the city were only

about 12 kilometers apart. The truck stopped and we got off, feeling strange standing in the center of the city. We began to walk the streets. The Germans, accustomed to the sight of prisoners in striped suits, did not glance at us. We decided to go into a café. We planned on sitting there, ordering coffee, and making ourselves comfortable, as if we were used to doing this in bygone days. But the waiter did not bother to come to our table! We looked around and not one of us said a word. Finally we were served cups of black coffee that tasted like the coffee at Magdeburg: bitter, watery, and cold. We took a can of tinned meat out of our knapsack, left it on the table and went on our way. Not one of us was a big hero alongside the Germans sitting in the café. We already regretted the trip to Weimar.

We walked slowly toward the city limits. We still wanted to do something. We decided to "commandeer" some special food for ourselves. There were one-story houses at the city's edge and we resolved to invade a house to demand something. The door was unlocked and we walked right in. We were astonished to see British army uniforms on hangers in the entrance hall. We had not recovered from the British presence there when a British officer burst in, took one look at us, and yelled hysterically: "Jews – out!"

It seemed that the Brit had had his fill of Jewish prisoners. At any rate, he had learned German very quickly.

Back at camp a surprise awaited us. In a German warehouse the American army had found a supply of textiles. They had taken the material to Weimar where it was used to sew clothes for us under American supervision. We were promised that we would all receive the clothes before leaving Buchenwald.

Each of us found ways to pass the days. Large groups of youth pursued SS men who were fleeing, but I was not interested in their success. I assumed that the liberating army would take care of the Nazis as it saw fit. What's more, I was not in great physical shape and could not chase after SS men. My main concern was to recover my health. I would still feel my ribs to check if there was any flesh on them. I doubted that I weighed more than the 29 kilo I had weighed immediately after the liberation, and I was suddenly very concerned about my health. The wound on my ankle had not yet healed and my gums were still bleeding. I wanted to be healthy; I was liberated and life outside was full of promise!

I could not take it all in. On my walks between the army barracks and the camp I would enter a block to try to see if I had the strength to climb up to the top bunk. I wanted to see whether my physical condition had improved. Sitting on the ground outside the block I could feel the clumps of earth under me. Examining my body I found that the pain came from my hip bones, which still did not have any flesh on them. Walking was less painful than sitting.

One morning a group of us decided to walk to the quarry at Buchenwald. We did not find the main route, so we took the paths through the mountains. Just two-three weeks ago prisoners who had worked here had carried stones on their backs like the Israelites in Egypt. Now the paths were deserted, as if it had all been a dream. No SS guards were to be seen in the green landscape. For the first time in a long while we could enjoy the spectacular vegetation. We had a desire to pick everything, but we were only looking for food and booty.

There was chaos at the quarry when we arrived. Hundreds of people were crowded into the space, most of them looking for real loot. A few days before the American army had dug an opening into a mountain cave.

Slowly, in single file, we went through the opening. We stayed in line out of habit and reached the cave entrance, which was very crowded. It was impossible to retreat so we all inched forward. The ceiling was low, the place was damp, and water dripped from the cave walls. Once inside we had to crawl on our hands and knees, scrounging and searching in the darkness.

I also scraped and searched, and found a leather strap from a wristwatch. Most of the "treasures" had been taken by those who had gotten there before me.

When we exited the cave we saw a crowd gathered around a merry group and we drew close. Gold sparkled from a knapsack. I fled from there wide-eyed from fear. That jewelry – could it have been my mother's?

The Americans distributed the new clothes. Real suits! A jacket and long pants made of thick army material! I was thrilled and filled with wonder at the Americans' great concern for us since liberation. The clothes fit us, with small adjustments. I did not let go of my striped clothes; I kept them in a knapsack to take with me when we left Buchenwald. I sewed the camp identification number on the front of my new jacket, as did many others. It was a kind of "hero's medal". We were walking around the camp and we were alive. Look at us, everyone!

I was a "political prisoner" with a red badge. According to rumors that spread through the camp, the US army planned to send all the young people from Buchenwald to recuperate in France. For that or for some other reason the camp's communist leadership organized the youth into groups. They gathered most of us into the SS halls, and for many long hours taught us Russian revolutionary songs, translated into many languages. After a few days I was tired of their lectures about the "new world" that would rise up in the old "homeland", that we would "return home and build a new egalitarian society together". With the exception of the piano that was playing nothing there attracted me. More than once I was told that I was a rebel against society, but to my joy they did not demand that I or anyone else participate in their meetings. Apparently they were concerned with the American command that did not support their organizing activities. Therefore I did not hesitate to turn them down and ignore their claims that I was inciting "rebellion" and "leading the others to corrupt ways", as one of the leaders put it. I told the communist leader that in

Hungary everyone was a fascist and that the Hungarians had cooperated with the Nazis. I was thrown out of the group, to the amusement of those present. Most of them never dreamed of returning to Eastern Europe.

The communist leaders even went further. They led a group of youth in a demonstration that marched to the command building of the American camp. No one took them seriously. I did not bother to find out how many were lured into joining the youth groups going back to their homelands.

The end of April, 1945

The American plan to move us out of Buchenwald began to take shape. We were informed that we would be leaving Buchenwald in two weeks. Several days later enrollment began. About 500 people from Block 66 signed up to go to France. We heard that Jewish organizations were also involved in this plan.

The days before the departure were very tense. At the beginning of May preparations for the large "peace rally" began. Journalists and military delegations were sent to Buchenwald to attend the ceremony that took place on May 8, 1945.

The "peace rally" that was held on the central parade grounds opposite the entrance gate, was impressive. I did not understand the speeches given in many languages. I understood the main message: that at its peak about 100,000 people were imprisoned in Buchenwald . There were 21,000 at the "peace rally", the remains of the camp. The American command reported that during the final days of the war many thousands were taken out of the camp, loaded onto cattle cars, and transported to the Dachau extermination camp. The war ended before they reached their destination. The SS men ran away to save their lives and left the cars closed. All the passengers in those cars were found dead. These were the thousands taken from the camp during the evacuation, which I had successfully escaped.

I assume that most of the *muselmänner* I had encountered at Buchenwald had not made it to Liberation Day. All camp commanders had claimed repeatedly, night and day, that: "this is not an extermination camp!", and in truth, everyone died a natural death, from starvation…

The Ukrainian groups marked the celebratory day by appearing in uniform: the leather clothes of the German armored corps, some stolen from the other prisoners. I was one of the few youth who were well acquainted with the Ukrainians, and my joy was complete. I knew I would never see these thugs again.

Preparations for leaving had been completed and we were ready to depart for France. In the Hungarian wing the communists continued their attempts to convince us to return to Hungary. They claimed that, "You stayed alive thanks to the communist leadership in Buchenwald!" As I saw it, the communists did not deserve any laurels or badges of honor. I didn't know what influence they had on daily life at Buchenwald, but we certainly knew that the food portions that had reached us in the invalids camp were much smaller than those in the upper camp - so in truth their claims was groundless. At any rate, the propagandists were not very successful, since the great majority of Block 66 inmates would not hear of returning to Hungary.

The departure from Buchenwald took place at the beginning of June. Passenger cars were provided for the children, the *Kinder Block*, and the trip to France began amidst great merriment. Our joy knew no bounds! Each car was assigned two leaders responsible for the safety of the passengers. It was total chaos. There was running back and forth between the cars throughout the trip. We could not get enough of the new-found luxuries!

Suddenly, not too long after we set out, someone shouted that he saw SS soldiers running freely in the area. With no warning we pulled the emergency brake and the train stopped.

Great commotion erupted in the train cars. Dozens got off the train and began chasing after unidentified people seen in the area of German factories, claiming they were pursuing SS soldiers. Of course no one was caught. It took a long time to get everyone back on the train and those in charge threatened that if people did not return immediately they would be left behind. Finally, everyone returned to the train and our journey continued.

What a wonderful feeling it was to be free to go wild! Those in charge could not contain us. We knew we had a long trip ahead of us until we reached Normandy in France, and we overflowed with happiness. We could not sit still. We all ran around talking to our friends, going from car to car until we had no strength left.

The engine slowed down. We went through a mountainous area with fruit orchards. It was cherry season. Again the emergency cord was pulled and the train stopped with a loud shudder. "Why did we stop? What happened?", asked the more naive ones among us.

There was no need for long explanations. Most of the passengers got off to pick cherries. We could see the German farmers in the distance running for their lives. They knew who the passengers were: in giant letters on the sides of the cars it said: "Buchenwald Concentration Camp".

This time no one looked for Germans, we only wanted cherries! The leaders screamed at us to come back and we slowly returned to the cars. The stronger boys managed to break off some big branches and brought them aboard. For many kilometers afterward we ate the cherries off the branches.

It took two days to travel through Germany before we arrived at the French border. The leaders went from car to car warning us not to get into any more mischief as we entered France, a friendly country. There was no need for explanations. For all our enthusiasm and need to vent our feelings, we knew that France would receive us as "camp survivors". As the train stopped at the first French town we were greeted with a warm reception, including a band. The scene repeated itself throughout the day.

I was impressed by the speed with which news of our arrival reached the French countryside. It is hard to explain the excitement that gripped us as we saw the receptions all along the way for the train with Jewish children from Buchenwald. In this country with its many vineyards, the bright green landscape of early summer, and the clear skies of Normandy with not a cloud in sight – we felt reborn.

We could not get enough of this new world. This is how freedom looked! We sat back on the upholstered seats as if we were the richest men on earth and looked out the train window at dense forests – everything was ours! I felt very well fed, although I could not remember what I ate first. Around me everyone patted their bursting stomachs. I remembered the words of the Frenchman from Block 66: "If we stay alive, we, the Christians, will take care to imprison all the Jews temporarily, until we get even with the Nazis! You Jews with your bible full of mercy will certainly forgive and forget too quickly!" I thought of him because of the satisfaction I felt in my new situation. Perhaps the Frenchman was right? I was not going to have time to worry about the Germans. Two days ago I saw the Frenchman along with everyone else chasing a suspicious German. And if we had caught such a German, what would I have done with him? I was even incapable of breaking a branch off a cherry tree.

I tried to fall asleep. I wanted so much to sleep, even to dream. Interestingly, I tried to remember the last time I had dreamed... Probably the time I had poured cement. Perhaps it was better this way. While we were rolling along, I continued to think, what would we do in France? I was sure of one thing: I wanted to remain among many people. Just this thought filled me with inexplicable confidence. Perhaps because I thought that if necessary I could always stoop down and hide behind the person in front of me. And another thought I had: would we be known as the *"Gruppe Buchenwald"* (Buchenwald Group) forever?

The others in the car began to run around. Very soon we would reach our final destination: Ecouis, the vacation village in Normandy. Such pampering! A free convalescent vacation.

"Bukenwald Hotel"

We arrived at the station in Ecouis, a small quiet village. It took a few days before we realized that there were only 250 villagers here, and there were 500 of us, the Buchenwald boys. The reception we received was fantastic. Together with the villagers, the organizers and the representatives of the OSE (Oeuvre de Secours aux Enfants), an organization that looked after war refugees, were there to receive us. All groups of boys were ushered into a huge block of buildings, into what had once been a seminary for priests. The buildings were gigantic with many rooms. A festive reception was prepared in the dining hall, the long tables set for us in the best of French tradition, including jugs of wine - a real novelty for us! We enjoyed all the goodies, with no limits imposed. Many of us were attracted to the wine and fought for the privilege of refilling the jugs in the dining room. After all, we should act as is proper in France!

Two days later we were assigned counselors whose job it was to keep us busy. It quickly became apparent that despite our age we were independent and very stubborn. The counselors found it difficult to keep us in line, and the feeling was that discipline was deteriorating. During the first days in Ecouis we spent a lot of time wandering through the fields around the village. We could not get enough. We ran through the entire village, and sometimes heard farmers complaining about: "the mob that had descended on our heads".

I reached Ecouis with a tattered but sturdy suitcase. Most of us had accumulated various items by the time we left Germany. My suitcase held all my possessions: two leather SS belts, a black SS hat, boxes of American cigarettes given to me by soldiers when I accompanied them on their visits of the invalids camp at Buchenwald, and the most impressive treasure of all: a pair of black pointed-toe patent-leather shoes. The shoes were huge but I took them with me thinking that I could trade them for something... I got them in the town of Erfurt, not far from the camp. After the liberation, the Erfurt municipality opened up distribution centers for prisoners freed from Buchenwald. As usual, I got there late. Only the large patent leather shoes were left, and I took them. Here in Ecouis anyone who wanted more wine would try to barter, but no one here wanted my shoes because of the pointed toes and the large size.

News of the children from Buchenwald spread through France. Many journalists arrived in Ecouis, including two Hungarian journalists stationed in Paris. I was amused by their efforts to convince me to return to "new Hungary". As far as I knew no one was persuaded to go back to Eastern Europe. Representatives from other countries also reached us, offering us the opportunity to sign up for a choice of immigration destinations. I knew that we were at Ecouis temporarily, and so I signed up to immigrate to several countries, including Palestine. Actually, I was convinced that the question of where I would go made no difference. I understood that there were so few Jews left that I would have to live among non-Jews wherever I went. The Jewish Agency had representatives alongside all the others. My friend Utzi, whose name I now realized was Ehud Walter, asked me if I had a Jewish name. "Of course", I answered, "my name is Moshe Yankel". Utzi told me that it was not a name, that in Palestine everyone had one Hebrew name. I told him not to worry about me, and that: "I had signed up to immigrate to every country. Whoever leaves here first, that's where I will go".

Utzi told me that there was news of an upcoming departure for Palestine for those who had relatives there. The British, who governed Palestine at the time, limited the number of immigrants, even those who survived the Holocaust, and demanded names of relatives, which posed an additional obstacle. He convinced me to give the Jewish Agency representative a made-up name of a relative in Palestine. We decided that the name of my new relative would be Berkovitch. My name was Zisovitch, and it sounded similar. Utzi accompanied me to registration. I gave the name with no twinge of conscience, and then I was asked where this Berkovitch lived. "Say Netanya" Utzi whispered, "It is a new city and it will be impossible to verify".

I did not pin much hope on the registration. I was still living each day as it came, without too many cares.

A few days later we had another surprise. A delegation from the Jewish Agency in Paris arrived amid great celebration. People from the Jewish Agency, and others whose positions we did not know, appeared before us in the large yard, informing us that they had come to draw up the final lists of the passengers for Palestine. We would need to be patient, because they needed to photograph each person who had registered in order to prepare passports.

I was thrilled by the thought that I would finally be going to a permanent place of residence. About 250 of us had signed up for this destination. The registration began in the morning, and was conducted alphabetically, which pushed my friend Utzi and me even further toward the end of the line. We wandered around impatiently while the registration proceeded slowly. Utzi was pleased with himself: "You see, we managed to outwit them and get you included in the list for aliya". I asked him to join me for a short hike in the neighborhood. We knew we had a few hours before it was our turn to register. We walked to the main road and saw a sign in French pointing toward a vacation village several kilometers away. Utzi grudgingly agreed to join me. I stopped an American army vehicle whose passengers identified us by the numbers sewn onto our jackets, and soon we were at the beach town.

Summer was just beginning. The beaches were full of vacationers and we wandered around aimlessly for several hours, feasting our eyes on the sight of the vacationers and enjoying the sense of freedom. There were lines at the local stores and bakeries. People were very courteous when they noticed us. They also recognized that we came from the death camps and urged us to proceed to the head of the line.

Time passed quickly when Utzi suddenly remembered that we had to get back to register. The way back to Ecouis was much more complicated as there was little traffic on the roads and we needed to catch a ride. We reached Ecouis towards evening and ran to the registration office where we learned that they had run out of film and registration had stopped.

I was indifferent to the situation. No one was really waiting for me in Palestine. We'll go next time. Utzi did not feel the same. He pleaded with the Jewish Agency officials, trying to convince them that he had to be included in the registration. "After all, I was born in Palestine!", he appealed persistently. The Jewish Agency officials were very forthcoming. They agreed to make room for us in the car and to take us to Paris with them in order to prepare the passports for us there. My friend had a hard time accepting my claim that it was thanks to me that we were going to Paris. I told him that: "Had it not been for the trip to the beach which I had proposed, we would not be visiting Paris".

The OSE people in Paris welcomed us with open arms. We lived like kings in Paris for one week. We were even taken on guided tours. In restaurants the owners would serve us, and most refused payment. This was a new feeling. Most of the French people we encountered identified with us and were friendly. Everywhere we went we felt their hatred towards the Germans.

Every day of freedom was a novelty for me. I could feel my body renewing itself. Utzi and I could not get enough fun and pleasure. Utzi knew some French and would ask questions at the historical sites. I asked him why he was interested in all the kings of France down through the ages. I told him that as far as I was concerned: "I am only looking for food stands, whatever is available!", but my friend, who was more mature than I was, told me that food for the mind was just as important. He went around with pen and paper in hand, copying all the dates from historical buildings. I tagged after him like a good student.

After a week the Jewish Agency informed us that we were to proceed to Marseilles since our group from Ecouis was being transferred to the immigration camp there. We left Paris regretfully. For me, the freedom we were granted by the OSE people and the money showered on us signified the true beginning of the period after the camps.

It was the beginning of July, and I was in Marseilles. The huts at the immigration camp in Marseilles were not particularly comfortable compared to the luxury we had enjoyed in Paris. However, with memories of the camps still fresh in our minds we had no difficulty adjusting to the new conditions. Food was plentiful, and for us that was the main thing. We all tended to join any line without asking what was being distributed.

Utzi and I would come and go as we pleased as we toured Marseilles. One time we were on one of Utzi's "educational sightseeing tours". At noon I announced that I would not continue on the tour with him, and we decided to go our separate ways and meet up at camp in the evening. I had enough money. I wandered around different parts of the city, especially attracted to the harbor area where wide steps led down to the water and stalls lined the flat areas between them. The scene was so enjoyable. I did not know French but nonetheless spent a pleasant afternoon which slipped into evening.

On the streets traffic was thinning out. I looked around and soon realized that I had taken a wrong turn and had no idea how to get to the immigration camp. I was already tired after a day of sightseeing and wanted to get back. But how could I without knowing French? Finally I hailed a buggy. "Where to?", asked the driver. "Buchenwald" I answered. The driver looked me over, and suddenly understood. His eyes shined with joy, "Bukenwald-hotel?" he asked. That is how the French pronounced the name. I nodded yes, got into the buggy and the trip through the streets of Marseilles began. He stopped on every street and asked, "Here?" The only word of French I knew was "*manger*", to eat. I drew a *Magen David* (Shield of David, a symbol of Jewish identity) on his buggy, pointing to it and then to myself. Somehow the driver found a small dry-goods store owned by Jews, and I found my salvation, a Jewish family who spoke Yiddish.

They understood immediately. They gave both of us dinner and made sure we were stuffed. I was now ready to return to the immigration camp, but as far as they were concerned the evening had just begun. There was no end to their questions: maybe I knew someone by this or that name? Perhaps I could identify a face among the many pictures they spread out for me to look at? They were from Poland. I was taken aback at their ignorance about the concentration camps, but did not have the emotional strength to recount everything that had come to pass there. I was stunned by their naïve reaction: How could it be that I did not remember the names of people who were with me in the camps? It felt strange looking at the photographs: family members of every age, dressed as if from a different world. I went through the family album politely, recalling similar pictures from my home, with the same clothes, from a different era.

As we parted I said to the very nice lady who was my hostess: "Don't be angry that I do not remember the people from the camps. Everyone there was thin, and we all wore striped uniforms".

The buggy driver accompanied me to the camp. I thanked him, glad to get back to the hubbub of the camp, asking again when we would leave and what had been distributed that I while I was away today. My friend Utzi had worried about me, afraid that I had gotten lost in the city. I told him that I had managed very well with my knowledge of French…

Preparations for our sailing were underway. We already knew the date and the name of the ship. The day finally arrived. It was a British ship named "*Mataroa*". I was filled with excitement boarding the ship. Everything was new and surprising, and there was no end to my questions: How many days would we be sailing? When would we arrive? I calmed down at the end of the first day. My questions were answered and my curiosity satisfied.

I cannot deny that what impressed me most was the service we received in the ship's dining room. In his black suit and a towel folded over his arm the British waiter went from table to table with a teapot and milk, offering endless cups of tea.

Several foreign passengers traveled with us on the ship. Their clothes were very colorful compared to the uniformity of the Buchenwald children's attire. In addition to the suit jacket with the number sewn across the chest, I had a pair of American army pants with many pockets that were too big on me, and I wore a leather belt with the SS emblem on it. I would not part with that belt for any amount of money on earth. Several times a day I would check the contents of all the pant pockets, happy with what I found. Of course none of us knew what the others kept in their pockets. We kept our "treasures" to ourselves: cigarettes, chewing gum, Buchenwald liberation papers, an identity card for the ship, and in a secret hiding place, a sizeable chunk of bread. No matter what happened, we were equipped with "emergency rations".

The voyage took one week. One morning we all went up to the ship's bridge. In the distance, through the fog, we could make out the shoreline of *"Eretz Israel"* (the Land of Israel). Our joy and enthusiasm knew no bounds. We had arrived at a new and unfamiliar world, a land where most of the inhabitants were Jews! Utzi was in seventh heaven; his dream had come true, this country was his birthplace. Part of his family would certainly be waiting for him when we arrived. Seeing his happiness my conscience began to bother me. Perhaps I had made my decision too hastily? Perhaps I had left members of my family back there? Perhaps someone was still alive after all? Perhaps I should have been less enthusiastic about the idea of coming to Eretz Israel? A million doubts plagued me, but I did not share them with a soul. Suddenly I remembered the name I had given when I registered to come to *Eretz Israel*: Berkovitch from Netanya. Actually, I had no one in this new land!

The noise and excitement of landing at Haifa swept me along. All my doubts gradually disappeared. The reception at Haifa was matter-of-fact and swift, and included glasses of milk and fresh rolls in abundance. On the buses the level of noise and excitement was high. Here and there complaints were heard about the hasty reception. Where was the brass band like the ones that welcomed us at the French train stations along the way to Ecouis in Normandy? Nothing here resembled those first days after the liberation.

The buses reached Camp Atlit. We were shaken by the sight of barbed wire fences around the camp, the endless rows of faded barracks in the giant camp and the armed British soldiers at the gate. Our enthusiasm and expectations about the new land plunged sharply. Needless to say it was hard to adjust to the familiar scene of barracks and barbed wire. We felt a sense of bitter indignation and aimed our cries at the British soldiers surrounding the camp.

Things calmed down gradually after extensive explanations from the immigration officials: "*Eretz Israel* was given to the British to govern as a mandate. Your legal immigration is an exception, granted to you only because you are the children of Buchenwald".

We were accustomed to changes in our living conditions, and I was reassured to hear that we would only be here for three days.

Registration for educational institutions and schools was conducted daily. Jewish Agency officials sat in the registration hall and assigned us according to political parties. I sat in front of a Jew with a full beard who wanted to know if my mother lit Shabbat candles and if I went to prayer on the Sabbath. My opinion on this issue was resolute: "My mother did indeed light Shabbat candles, and I had even studied in a *cheder*", I screamed at the man, "but ever since my last argument with He who sits in the Heavens, when I poured out my prayers to him and my supplications went unanswered, I decided to study in a regular school!"

8.

Afterword

On July 17, 1945, together with a group of Buchenwald children, I arrived at the agricultural school in Magdiel. I will forever treasure the Magdiel educational institution. The warmth we received, and the feeling that we belonged, cannot be put in words. There were also dark days at Magdiel, when I regretted the hasty decision I had made to immigrate to Israel. I was young, and I knew that my father had been murdered, but perhaps I should have stayed to search for other members of our family who may have survived?

Two years later, in 1947, I received the happy news that my sister Koti was alive and had arrived in Palestine. I rushed to meet her at the detention camp in Atlit. She told me that she and my mother had reached Auschwitz. My mother was sent to the gas chambers in the selection. My sister was sent to a labor camp, and was liberated after the war from the Theresienstadt concentration camp.

After the war my sister had returned to Hungary to search for remaining members of the family. She found my name on a list of survivors the community committee had compiled, but no one knew where I was.

My sister was married in Budapest, and along with her husband and his sister and brother-in-law decided to immigrate to *Eretz Israel*. In a displaced persons camp in Italy they were told that I was definitely in *Eretz Israel*. That is why they sailed on the illegal immigration ship *"Bracha Fuld"* in order to reach *Eretz Israel*. However the ship was captured by the British and its passengers exiled to Cyprus. That is where my sister's first child was born. When they finally arrived in Israel and were released from Camp Atlit, their suffering also came to an end.

Here my story comes to an end, and the vision of the prophet Ezekiel is fulfilled:

Because we were as dry bones,

with only a spark of life remaining.

And here, we rose up with a new spirit in us.

And you there, sons of Satan,

Accursed murderers of Auschwitz!

You who sent the bodies and souls of my loved ones up the chimneys of Auschwitz-Birkenau

You, who fertilized your accursed land with the ashes of my loved ones,

May you be cursed for all eternity.

To my dear parents:

I will keep my promise to be your *Kaddish:* [28]

Yit gadal v'yit kadash sh'mei raba

Moshe Ziv (Zisovitch)

Bnei Zion

December 1991

---

[28] *Kaddish* - the Jewish prayer traditionally recited in memory of the dead.

Glossary

Bar Mitzvah - a coming of age Jewish ritual when a Jewish boy turns 13.

Blockälteste - (block elder) - a prisoner functionary whose duties were to maintain order and discipline in the block, distribute food and keep records of the prisoners. The block elders had almost unlimited power over the prisoners.

Blockmaster - block or barrack leader.

Challah - traditional Jewish bread, usually braided and typically eaten on ceremonial occasions such as the Sabbath and major Jewish holidays.

Cheder - A Jewish religious classroom where Jewish boys study Judaic texts and Hebrew.

Hitler Jugend - The Hitler Youth, the youth organization of the Nazi Party in Germany.

Kaddish - the Jewish prayer traditionally recited in memory of the dead.

Kapo - a prisoner in a Nazi concentration camp assigned by the SS guards to supervise forced labor or to carry out administrative tasks. Part of the SS prisoner functionary system.

The prisoner functionary system was comprised of prisoners who supervised or carried out administrative functions. This saved costs by allowing camps to function with fewer SS personnel. Prisoner functionaries had access to certain privileges such as civilian clothes, and were spared the atrocities suffered by the regular prisoners, provided they performed their duties to the satisfaction of the SS functionaries.

The important functionary positions inside the camp included the Lagerälteste (camp leader or camp senior) and the Blockälteste (block or barracks leader or senior).The Blockälteste (block or barracks leader) had to ensure that rules were followed in the individual barracks, and was also responsible for the prisoners in the barracks.

Kislev - the third month of the Jewish calendar.

Kosher - foods that conform to a set of Jewish religious dietary laws. In slang may also mean "proper" or "legitimate".

Kvitel - a note written by an individual with a petitionary prayer given to the Rabbi in order to receive is blessing.

Lagerälteste - camp leader or camp senior.

Lagerführer - the head SS officer assigned to a particular concentration camp who served as the commander of the camp.

Lauskontrolle - lice inspection and control.

Ma'ariv - evening prayer in Judaism.

Meister - German citizen who was responsible for a specific job in the factory.

Muselmänner - a slang term used to refer to prisoners exhibiting a combination of emaciation and weakness from starvation and an apathetic listlessness, and who had lost contact with reality and spent each day rocking back and forth like a Muslim at prayer.

"Maoz tzur yeshuati…"- Rock of Ages, a song sung during

the Jewish holiday Hanukkah, which is celebrated around the time of Christmas.

Peyes or payot - the sidelocks of ultra-Orthodox men and boys, in keeping with the Torah's prohibition of shaving the "corners" of the head.

Rabbinate - the rabbinical authority of Judaism in Israel that has jurisdiction over many aspects of Jewish life in Israel, including Jewish burial.

Rosh Hashanah - Jewish New Year.

Shema Yisroel - Hear O'Israel, is considered the most important part of the prayer service in Judaism.

Stube-dienst - a kapo's assistant.

Tefillin (also called phylacteries) - a set of small black leather boxes containing scrolls of parchment inscribed with verses from the Torah. They are attached to the body with leather straps and worn by Orthodox Jewish men on their head and arm during weekday morning prayers.

Yiddish - a Germanic language and the language of central and eastern European Jews.

Made in the USA
Middletown, DE
27 August 2019